Loving God With All
Five Senses

Tammy B. Melton

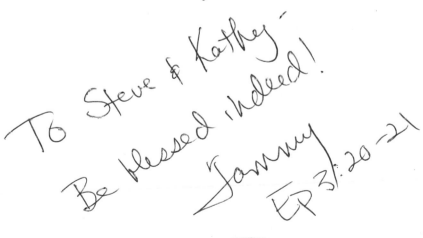

To Steve & Kathey -
Be blessed indeed!
Tammy
EP 3:20-21

xulon
PRESS

Dedication

This book is written in memory of my grandmother, Margaret Flanders Barron. Grandmother lived with our family from the time I was 2 until she went home to be with the Lord when I was a sophomore in college. She had such an impact on my life for Christ. Grandmother was the one God chose to lead me to the Lord in prayer when I was 4 years old. I learned so many things about ministry by observing this godly woman as she led children's crusades, ministered to ladies in women's ministry, prayed with individuals at the altar, spoke behind the pulpit, and so much more. She even taught me how to sing alto! I will always be grateful to God for blessing me with Grandmother. I look forward to the day when we are reunited in Heaven!

Acknowledgements

To my beloved husband, Bill Melton – Words cannot express my appreciation for your love and support. Besides salvation with Jesus, marrying you was absolutely the best decision of my life! You're the best!

To my lovely daughters, Amy and Amber – What a joy to be your mother! Thank you for your patience with me as I spent so many hours preparing this book. I pray that you will both love God with all five senses the rest of your lives!

To my extended family, the Barrons and the Meltons - I love all of you! I especially want to thank my parents, Don and Lorene Barron, for bringing me up with such a Godly heritage. I will never take that for granted.

To my church family, Trinity Fellowship in Sharpsburg, Georgia, especially my pastor and his wife, Mark and Julie Anthony - You will never know how much your support of my ministry means to me. Thank you, Trinity family!

To my Servanthood Ministries family – I especially am grateful for you, Nancy Stow, my mentor! I am honored to hold my credentials for ministry through Servanthood. I am so grateful for my Servanthood sisters and brothers for being there for me at every level of ministry. I love you all!

To all those who support Legacy Ministries – This book would not have been written without your prayers and support. Thank you so much for praying me through!

To Tori Stigleman – I am so thankful for you! I prayed for a personal assistant, and God blessed me with you! Thank you from the bottom of my heart!

To Sharon Hodge – Thank you so much for the hours you poured into editing this book! Your insight and help was priceless!

To Mary Frances Bowley and Wellspring Living – Thank you for allowing me to partner with you in ministry. I sincerely enjoyed teaching this book to the girls in the home. Girls, you are truly trophies of God's grace!

To My Lord and Savior – This is by far the most important acknowledgement! Lord, without You I am nothing! I am so blessed and privileged to have been chosen by You to write this book. Loving You is absolutely the one desire of my heart; all the other desires stem out of that! You never cease to amaze me!

"*Loving God With All Five Senses* is an excellent study for one new in their Christian walk and those who have been in the faith for some years. In our hectic lives sometimes we lose sight of how uniquely we were created by Him. Every fiber of our being speaks of God's care and creativity. Relating the five senses to our spiritual walk has been captured in this study. I especially appreciate the 'Going Deeper' sections which give interaction with the Word and text."

Nancy Stow, President, Servanthood Ministries, New Boston, TX
www.servanthoodministries.com

"*Loving God with All Five Senses* is a book that will motivate you toward intimacy with the Father in ways you have never considered. Tammy's teachings have been a catalyst for amazing transformation to those I know who have read the book and worked through the exercises. This is a MUST READ for anyone who desires to experience intimacy with God in broader and fuller dimensions."

Mary Frances Bowley, author of *League of Dangerous Women*
Director of Wellspring Living, Inc.
www.wellspringliving.org

"Tammy Melton writes to the world of God's great love for us. God desires for us to feast on His Word. *Loving God With All Five Senses* is a daily tasting of this encouragement. I challenge you to discover what Tammy has written within these pages. It is a must read!"

Ann Platz: author of *Queen Esther's Reflection*
www.annplatz.com

"Tammy Melton has done a masterful job linking the five senses to the cultivation of an intimate relationship with God. These provocative concepts can become practical and relevant by using her 'Going Deeper' Bible study at the end of each chapter. This book is a must read for the growing Christian!"

Dick Biggs, Author of *Burn Brightly Without Burning Out*
www.biggspeaks.com

"*Loving God with All Five Senses* is a fresh approach to encouraging the believer's spiritual growth and intimacy with God. Living in the material world as we do, we relate to our environment through our five physical senses. After reviewing how these senses function in the physical realm, Tammy then adeptly explains the spiritual analogy of each one. I recommend this book both for personal use and for group Bible studies."

Ruthanne Garlock
co-author, *Lord, I Need to Pray with Power*

Table of Contents

Preface

Have you ever wondered what it would take to satisfy your deepest longing? We all have an innate desire to get to know our Creator (Psalm 63:1 and Psalm 84:2). Not only do we want to know Him, but our Creator also desires an intimate relationship with each and every one of us! Zephaniah 3:17 (NIV) says, "The Lord your God is with you, he is mighty to save. He will take great delight in you, he will quiet you with his love, he will rejoice over you with singing."

Our yearning to know our Creator starts with a desire to know what our purpose is. Many people want God to reveal His will for their life, but they do not spend time seeking Him. Instead of setting their heart on knowing His will, they must first set their heart on simply getting to know Him (Matthew 6:33). In John 14:6 Jesus said, "I am the way, the truth and the life." Yes, God offers us eternal life in Heaven through Jesus, but He also wants us to have a life of peace and joy on earth. Do you want to know the way for your life, the truth that sets you free, and how to find a more abundant life? Then you must get to know Jesus.

It is sad to say that many who are sitting in the church pews do not know God. The term "Christian" is often used very loosely. When I ask people if they know Jesus, I get various responses. Instead of a direct answer to my question, I often hear, "I go to church." Sometimes they cannot even tell me the name of the church they attend! Some people in America think they are Christians simply because this nation was founded on Christian principles. They are

Americans, therefore they think they are Christians. Others think that they are Christians because their parents took them to church when they were growing up. In the second part of John 14:6 Jesus said, *"No man comes to the Father but by me."* If you wonder if you are a Christian, simply call out to Jesus. There is not a formula prayer for becoming a Christian. It is a matter of the heart. If you truly want to know Jesus, tell Him! Acknowledge your need for a savior, confess your sins to Him and ask Him to come into your heart and life.

As you get to know Jesus and learn how to "dwell in the secret place of the Most High" (Psalm 91:1), two things will happen. First, little by little and step by step, your character will change to become more Christ-like. Second, God will begin to teach you what it means to trust and follow Him. Then you will begin to know His will for your life, and you will also be prepared to walk it out. The fruit of the Spirit will begin to manifest itself in your life. (Galatians 5:22-23: "The fruit of the Spirit is love, joy, peace, longsuffering, kindness, goodness, faithfulness, gentleness, and self-control.") When that happens, through Him you will do mighty things! Daniel 11:32b says, "...the people who know their God shall be strong, and carry out great exploits."

It seems as though God is stirring people in the church to have an intimate relationship with Him like never before. Yes, throughout the ages He has called individuals as well as groups to get to know Him on a personal level. But as time draws closer to the "blessed hope" of the church, when Jesus comes to get His bride, God's beckoning is sounding louder (Titus 2:13). Finally, some of us are starting to get it! He is preparing us to be a church "without spot or wrinkle" at the time of His appearing (Ephesians 5:27).

I remember thinking as a young person growing up in a Christian home, "How in the world is God going to get the church to be 'without spot or wrinkle'?" I am beginning to see that it is through this wooing to intimacy with Him. When you make sacrifices to seek God and to spend intimate time with Him, you will make it your aim to please Him. Each time you seek God, another spot will fade and another wrinkle will be ironed out. As more and more Christians yield to God's wooing, their individual fires will unite and cause a bonfire. Watch out! When this happens, we will experience more than revival! The gospel will blanket the earth, and the church finally will be ready to be declared "without spot or wrinkle."

Yes, we have read and heard teachings about having an intimate relationship with God in books, during sermons, conferences and retreats. But now it is time to "be doers of the Word and not hearers only" (James 1:22). It is my desire that God will use this Bible study on loving God with all five senses to help you cross that line. My prayer for you comes from Ephesians:

> "When I think of the wisdom and scope of God's plan, I fall to my knees and pray to the Father, [15] the Creator of everything in heaven and on earth. [16] I pray that from his glorious, unlimited resources he will give you mighty inner strength through his Holy Spirit. [17] And I pray that Christ will be more and more at home in your hearts as you trust in him. May your roots go down deep into the soil of God's marvelous love. [18] And may you have the power to understand, as all God's people should, how wide, how long, how high, and how deep his love really is. [19] May you experience the love of Christ, though it is so great you will never fully understand it. Then you will be filled with the fullness of life and power that comes from God."
>
> Ephesians 3:14-19 (NLT)

Introduction

⟡

God is calling Christians to intimacy with Him. Many times, however, the temptation to satisfy the desires of our five senses hinders an intimate relationship with our Creator. *Loving God with All Five Senses* shows how amazingly God created our physical bodies. Our senses help us enjoy our world, as well as help protect us. With the understanding of how our five senses work, we can gain a perspective that promotes a thriving, personal relationship with God, as well as healthy relationships with others.

Loving God with All Five Senses is a combination book and Bible study. The book is divided into six units—an introductory unit and one unit for each of the five senses. This six-week study is designed to be read one chapter a day, five days each week. The reader is taken on a spiritual journey that starts on the first day by learning how God created us with the particular sense covered in the unit. The information on the physical sense is then used as a link to the spiritual, with the last day of each unit always covering the spiritual aspect the particular sense represents. The second day of each unit covers how misuse of the sense in the physical hinders the development of what the sense represents in the spiritual. Each day has an easy-to-read chapter followed by an in-depth Bible study called "Going Deeper," which can be explored for further study or skipped to be done at a later time.

The following chart shows how our physical senses relate to our spiritual senses:

Taste	Desire/Passion
Touch	Worship
Sight	Vision
Hearing	Faith
Smell	Discernment

This book presents practical applications for everyday life, as well as keys to developing a deeper walk with God. People at all levels of spiritual maturity have been positively impacted by *Loving God with All Five Senses.*

First Things First

*"But seek first the kingdom of God and His righteousness,
and all these things shall be
added to you." Matthew 6:33*

Day 1

We Are Fearfully and Wonderfully Made!

"In the beginning God created the heavens and the earth."
Genesis 1:1

Only God can create something out of nothing. The world was created by God's spoken words. When God created man, however, He took time to form him with His hands. "And the Lord God formed man of the dust of the ground, and breathed into his nostrils the breath of life; and man became a living being" (Genesis 2:7).

Not only did God form the first man, but He also formed each of us in our mother's wombs. In Jeremiah 1:5 God said, "Before I formed you in the womb I knew you…" Below is a list, used by permission, from the National Right to Life website that shows the development of a fetus in the womb:

Day 1: Fertilization: All human chromosomes are present; unique human life begins.

Day 22: Heart begins to beat with the child's own blood, often a different type than the mother's.

Week 3: By the end of third week the child's backbone, spinal column and nervous system are forming. The liver, kidneys and intestines begin to take shape.

Week 5: Eyes, legs and hands begin to develop.

Week 6: Brain waves are detectable; mouth and lips are present; fingernails are forming.

Week 7: Eyelids and toes form; nose is distinct. The baby is kicking and swimming.

Week 8: Every organ is in place, bones begin to replace cartilage, and fingerprints begin to form. By the 8th week the baby can begin to hear.

Weeks 9 and 10: Teeth begin to form; fingernails develop. The baby can turn his head and can frown. The baby can hiccup.

Weeks 10 and 11: The baby can "breathe" amniotic fluid and urinate. Week 11 the baby can grasp objects placed in its hand; all organ systems are functioning. The baby has a skeletal structure, nerves and circulation.

Week 12: The baby has all of the parts necessary to experience pain, including nerves, spinal cord and thalamus. Vocal cords are complete. The baby can suck its thumb.

Week 14: At this age the heart pumps several quarts of blood through the body every day.

Week 15: The baby has an adult's taste buds.

Month 4: Bone marrow is now beginning to form. The heart is pumping 25 quarts of blood a day. By the end of month 4 the baby will be 8-10 inches in length.

Week 17: The baby can have dream (REM) sleep.

Months 5 and 6: The baby practices breathing by inhaling amniotic fluid into its developing lungs. The baby will grasp at the umbilical cord when it feels it. Most mothers feel an increase in movement, kicking and hiccups from the baby. Oil and sweat glands are now functioning. The baby is now 12 inches long or more, and weighs up to one and a half pounds.

Months 7 through 9: Eyeteeth are present. The baby opens and closes his eyes. The baby is using four of the five senses (vision, hearing, taste and touch.) He knows the difference between waking and sleeping, and can relate to the moods of the mother. The baby's skin begins to thicken, and a layer of fat is produced and stored beneath the skin. Antibodies are built up, and the baby's heart begins to pump 300 gallons of blood per day. Approximately one week before the birth the baby stops growing and "drops," usually head down, into the pelvic cavity.[1]

The development of a baby inside a mother's womb is incredible beyond words. So also is the continued development of the body after birth, throughout childhood and into adulthood. Birth is just the beginning of an incredible journey of growth and development in this life on earth.

As Christians, our walk with the Lord begins with faith. Throughout our new life in Christ, true faith is a continuous journey of walking with God and growing in Him. Hebrews 11:1 says that "faith is the substance of things hoped for, the evidence of things not seen." Although we cannot see what will happen down the road of life, our faith in Jesus will carry us through—not because of how faithful we are, but because of how faithful He is.

According to verse 6 in that same chapter, "without faith it is impossible to please Him, for he who comes to God must believe that He is, and that He is a rewarder of those who diligently seek Him." We cannot merely believe in God, we must also believe that He will reward us when we seek to know Him. When we seek God through prayer, Bible study and taking time to listen for His voice, we demonstrate the kind of faith that pleases God.

Whether or not we realize it, our need for spiritual fulfillment is greater than any other need we have (Matthew 4:1-4; Matthew 6:24-33). When we stop serving Christ with mediocrity and begin to seek God with our whole mind, heart and soul, we will find true fulfillment. I pray that you will experience a glimpse of this as you continue in this Bible study.

Going Deeper

God the Creator

> *"In the beginning God created the heavens and the earth."*
> *Genesis 1:1*

It is interesting to note that the Hebrew word here for "create" is *bara'*. According to Vine's Complete Expository Dictionary, "This verb is of profound theological significance since it has only God as its subject. Only God can 'create' in the sense implied by *bara'*. The verb expresses creation out of nothing, an idea seen clearly in passages having to do with creation on a cosmic scale. All other verbs for 'creating' allow a much broader range of meaning; they have both divine and human subjects, and are used in contexts where bringing something or someone into existence is not the issue."[2]

Read Colossians 1:16. What does this verse say that God created?

For whom did He create them?

The opening verses of the Gospel of John are about Jesus. Verse 1 states that Jesus, the Word, is God. What does John 1:3 say about Jesus and creation?

Read Revelation 4:11. According to this verse, the Lord is worthy to receive glory, honor and power because He created all things. For what reason does it say He created all things?

Read Jeremiah 10:11-12. No other god made the heavens and the earth. What does verse 11 say will happen to the other gods?

Write verse 12.

What does Romans 11:36 say?

As we saw in the opening of *Going Deeper*, only God can create something out of nothing. Nothing is impossible with God (Luke 1:37). When we are in the midst of a trial from which escape seems impossible, God can make a way!

Write out Hebrews 11:3 and turn your faith toward God!

We Are Fearfully and Wonderfully Made!

When we as humans make something, we take pride in our work and take great care of our creation. How much more does God take pride in us and care for us?

Read Psalm 139 and meditate on what this is telling you about what God thinks of you.

Read Luke 12:6-7 and answer the following questions:
Verse 6 – What does this say that God has not forgotten?

Verse 7 – What does this say God knows about us?

This should remind us not to worry, because we are more valuable to God than the sparrows are!

Prayer

Lord, as Your Word says in Psalm 139:14, "I will praise You, for I am fearfully and wonderfully made; marvelous are Your works, and that my soul knows very well." You formed me in my mother's womb, and therefore You love and care about me more than I can ever imagine! I pray that I really would *know* that very well. Please forgive me for the times I have not been satisfied with the characteristics of my body or personality. Forgive me for the times when I have not taken care of myself physically or spiritually. Forgive me for the times I have cared more about what people think of my appearance than I care about what You think about me. I want to grow in wisdom and stature (Luke 2:52) to be all that You have designed me to be. In Jesus' Name, Amen!

First Things First

Day 2

Don't Let the Flesh Get in the Way of the Spirit!

G od uses the physical as a model for the spiritual. All of the Old Testament feasts point to Christ. The Passover is a familiar example of this (1 Corinthians 5:7b).[1] Types and foreshadows in the Old Testament are physical things that represent the spiritual. The author of Hebrews talks of the tabernacle being a picture of Heaven. In that same way, the five senses with which He has blessed us in the physical body are representations of what we can have in the spiritual realm. *Not only do the five senses of the outer man represent those characteristics of the inner man, but often times the way we use the five senses can hinder or promote the development of those spiritual characteristics.*

Our awesome Creator intricately made us with the five senses of taste, touch, sight, hearing and smell. It is amazing to think about the many details that are involved in each sense. God wants us to experience each sense fully and wondrously. He created our senses to help us enjoy life, as well as to protect us as we avoid things that are not pleasing to our senses. The problem is that in our sinful human nature, we tend to overindulge in the desires of our senses. We can be so self-focused that we start worshipping created things—physical beauty, luxurious material possessions and such—instead of our Creator (Romans 1:25).

God is stirring His church to intimacy with Him more than ever before. It is the theme of sermons, books and Christian music. In order to attain intimacy with Christ, we must go beyond the five senses, or the natural realm. We must not be distracted by what our physical bodies want.

We need to remember that there is so much more than what we see with the natural eye and what we feel with our natural hands. There is a supernatural realm. That is where faith comes in, and we find Jesus! "Now faith is the substance of things hoped for, the evidence of things not seen" (Hebrews 11:1).

The Bible encourages us to "look not at the things that are seen, but at the things which are not seen. For the things which are seen are temporary, but the things which are not seen are eternal" (2 Corinthians 4:18). We cannot do this on our own, because "... the natural man does not receive the things of the Spirit of God, for they are foolishness to him; nor can he know them, because they are spiritually discerned" (1 Corinthians 2:14).

It is when we finally surrender our lives to Christ and ask Him to be the Lord of our lives that the Holy Spirit comes and dwells in us. Jesus said of the Holy Spirit, "I will pray the Father, and He shall give you another Comforter, that he may abide with you forever" (John 14:16 KJV). In the same chapter He went on to say, "...the Comforter, which is the Holy Spirit, whom the Father will send in my name, He shall teach you all things, and bring all things to your remembrance, whatsoever I have said unto you" (John 14:26).

Before beginning the study on how we can love God through each sense, it will help to compare the natural and supernatural realms. The Bible has much to say about living in the spirit as opposed to living in the flesh. If we just look to the physical senses for gratification, we will be walking down a path that leads to death. However, if our primary focus is beyond the flesh to the spirit, we will have an abundant life here on earth that leads to joy for eternity with Christ!

If we are concerned only with the natural realm of this physical body, without considering the needs of soul and spirit, we will end up in a futile cycle of tending to the needs of our bodies, without any lasting satisfaction. We may try whipping our bodies into shape through means of diet and exercise, or we may try to indulge in satisfying the cravings of the body through the five senses. All the while, the void in the core of our being grows.

It is an interesting phenomenon that when we walk not according to the flesh, but according to the Spirit, every part of us—spirit, soul, and body—comes into alignment. Our spirits experience God's presence, and we are transformed by the renewing of our minds. We make right choices that allow our emotions to be settled. When this happens, our bodies will be healthy, free of stress-induced sickness! Then, and only then, can we experience what Jesus was talking about when He said, "Peace I leave with you, my peace I give to you; not as the world gives do I give to you. Let not your heart be troubled, neither let it be afraid" (John 14:27).

Going Deeper

Flesh versus Spirit

We reap what we sow. If we sow into our flesh, or carnal nature, the things we reap will be temporary and will lead to destruction. If we sow into our spirit, what we reap will bring rewards on earth, and abundant life eternally. Read the following scriptures and answer the questions.

Matthew 26:41 – What do we need to do so that we do not fall into temptation?

What part of us is willing?   What part of us is weak?

Note: This is exactly why we need to set aside more time to feed and exercise our spirits! If this is important to us, we will. When we do, we will be able to escape temptation more readily.

John 3:6 – What does our flesh give birth to?
What does the Spirit give birth to?

John 6:63 – What does the Spirit do?
What does the flesh profit?
What did Jesus say about His Words?

Galatians 5:16-17 – What does verse 16 say about living by the Spirit?

What does verse 17 say about the sinful nature in relation to the Spirit?

Galatians 6:8 – What do you need to do if you want to reap eternal life and not destruction?

Pause right now and ask the Lord what you are doing in your life right now that is "sowing to please the flesh" and what you need to do to "sow to please the Spirit."

Read Romans 8:1-17 and answer the following questions:
Verse 1 – Who gets to experience a life with no condemnation?

What is condemnation to you? (You might want to look it up in the dictionary.)

Verse 2 – What has made us free from the law of sin and death?

Verse 3 – The Old Testament law (Ten Commandments) did not offer us hope, it just made us aware of sin. It let us know of our need for a Savior. Because of that, what did God do?

Verse 4 – In whom will the righteous requirement of the law be fulfilled?

Verse 5 – What do those who live according to the flesh set their mind on?

What do those who live according to the spirit set their mind on?

Verse 6 – What does this verse call death?
What does it call life and peace?

Verse 7 – What does this say about the sinful, or carnal mind?

Verse 8 – Who cannot please God?

Verse 9 – How can we be in the Spirit and not in the flesh?

Verse 10 – If Christ is in us, our bodies may die, but what about our spirits?

Verse 11 – What did the Spirit do for Jesus?
What will the Spirit do for us?

Verses 12-13 – If we live according to the flesh what will happen?

If we live according to the Spirit what will happen?

Verses 14-16 – How do we know we are children of God?

Verse 17 – GOOD NEWS!! We are not only children of God, but we are _____

God's adoption of us into His family as His heirs is the ultimate result of true intimacy with Christ! I am excited that you have chosen to join me on this journey as we experience loving God with all five senses!

Prayer

Dear Lord, I pray that I will become more aware of my spiritual senses as opposed to just being concerned with my physical senses of taste, touch, sight, hearing and smell. I know that the only way this will happen is if You are in my life! I invite You into the very core of my being! I want to lay aside the desires of my flesh and embrace Your desires for my spirit, soul and body. Please show me those areas of my life where I am not surrendered to You. Help me to be willing to let them go. Thank You for Your Word that says if I seek You first, all the other areas of my life will be fulfilled, and I will experience abundant life! (See Matthew 6:33 and John 10:10b.)

First Things First

Day 3

The Gates of Hell Shall Not Prevail!

In Bible times, perimeter walls around cities were important for protection from enemy attacks. Guards were strategically placed at the gates to monitor all who entered and exited the city. Governing officials held planning meetings at city gates. Gates also were where kings met with the people, prophets gave words from the Lord, tribunals occurred, and the people even set up market.[1]

In Matthew 16:18 Jesus declared that "the gates of hell shall not prevail against" the church. Any strategies Satan and his governing officials have planned against us shall not prevail! Nothing the enemy tries to do to us can separate us from Christ's love. In the midst of every attack, we are more than conquerors through Jesus! (See Romans 8:37-39.)

Sometimes the enemy tries to put walls around us to keep us from receiving all that God has for us. He even sets up shop at the gates by selling us a bill of goods in the form of lies that lead to destruction! We cannot let him! It has been said that our minds are Satan's playground. If we ever see signs that the enemy has set up camp in our minds, we must cry out to God. If we submit to God, then we can resist the devil and he will flee (James 4:7). If the wall is already a fortress, God can destroy those walls just as He did the walls of Jericho, in Joshua 6.

The children of Israel, led by the priests carrying the Ark of the Covenant[2], had just crossed the Jordan River on dry ground. The time of wandering in the wilderness was finally over. They were entering a new season of their lives. They were going to possess the

31

land God had promised them—a land flowing with milk and honey! God told them to set up 12 stones (one for each of the tribes of Israel) as a memorial. This memorial was to remind the children of Israel how God brought them over the Jordan River on dry ground just as he had done forty years earlier when Moses led the Israelites out of slavery in Egypt by crossing the Red Sea on dry ground.

Can you imagine the joy and thanksgiving the Israelites felt? They had just been freed from a wilderness season to inherit the Promised Land. They may not have known that even though God's presence was with them, and they were released to inherit the land, warfare was just around the corner. The enemy does not stop fighting us when we receive Christ's presence into our lives. In fact, the more effective we are for Christ, the more Satan will try to thwart God's purposes for us.

The first city the children of Israel came to, Jericho, had to be conquered. (When God leads us into "land" he has promised us, He will go before us and drive out all the previous inhabitants!) God commanded His people to march in silence once around the city wall each day for six days. On the seventh day He commanded them to march around the wall seven times. On the seventh time, the priests were to blow shofars (rams' horns), and the people were to shout. Again, the Ark of the Covenant preceded the people. As long as God's presence was with them, they were protected! The Bible says that on the seventh time around Jericho, the priests blew the shofars, the people shouted, and the wall fell down flat!

Nowhere else in scripture did God ask his people to march around the enemy seven times, blow rams' horns and shout. When we have Jericho walls that need to come down, we need to seek God and get clear direction from Him on how the walls will come down. Whatever God says happens! That means that as we obey His commands, just as the Israelites did, those walls the enemy has built to keep us from being all that God has called us to be must fall flat to the ground!

Jesus destroyed Satan's power when He died on the cross and rose from the dead! The enemy does not have authority over a Christian who accepts Jesus' atonement. Since the devil does not have authority, he operates in deception. The Bible says that Satan is a liar and the father of all lies (John 8:44). If Satan can get someone to believe a lie, that person will be bound and unproductive.

Only knowing God's truth will set us free. As we seek His truth, the Bible promises that we will find it (Matthew 7:7-8). Truth is foundational to a successful walk with God. That is why the "belt of truth" is the first piece of the armor God tells us to put on in Ephesians 6:10-17. As we find God's truth and apply it to our lives, *everything else will work out!* (See Matthew 6:33.)

Going Deeper

Satan, the deceiver

Satan is very sly. Sometimes he tries to get you to question what God has said and to twist God's words to mean something that is not true. He did that to Eve in the Garden of Eden.

Read Genesis 2:16-17 and Genesis 3:1-6. Compare them to answer the following questions.

Genesis 3:1-6:
Verse 1 – Satan, being sly, came in the form of a serpent. What was the difference between what Satan said and what God had previously said?

Verses 2 & 3 – Sometimes *we* add to what God tells us. Compare Eve's response of what God had said with Genesis 2:16-17. What did she add to what God said?

Verses 4 & 5 – The devil will try to make you think that God is a liar, and then he will try to tempt you. Satan said outright that God was wrong. He then began to give Eve words to entice her to sin.

Verse 6 – This verse showed that Eve really considered what the serpent told her. She ended up taking his bait and followed through with the temptation to act against God's word. When Satan messes with our minds, we need to dismiss it. The longer we ponder the enemy's words, the more we will be tempted, and the greater the odds will be that we will give in to the temptation to sin.

Nothing Can Separate us from Christ's Love!

Just as the Israelites were preceded on their travels in the desert by God's manifest presence in the Ark of the Covenant, we also have the presence of God. The difference is that we have access to the presence of the Almighty God within us! (See 1 Corinthians 3:16.)

Read Romans 8:35-39. Underline and meditate on verses 38-39.

Walls that Hinder Healthy Relationships

Not only does Satan try to build walls to keep us from a relationship with God, he also tries to erect walls around us to keep us from experiencing healthy relationships with other people.

According to the last part of Galatians 5:6, what really matters in our Christian walk?

In Galatians 5:14, what does it say is the fulfillment of God's law?

Read 1 John 4:7-8. In verse 7, what does it say about one who loves? What does verse 8 say about one who does not show love to others?

These verses show how important it is for us to love people whom God puts into our lives. This is why the devil desires to put up walls between us so that we will not love each other. He wants us to be ineffective Christians. Whether it is between races, genders, denominations, family members, co-workers, or neighbors, the enemy works overtime to put walls between people. Write a prayer asking God to take down any walls between you and others and to let you know specific ways you can show love to them.

Prayer

Father, God, Your love is greater than any wall the enemy can build against me. I thank You that the strategies he has planned against me will not prevail as long as my life is built with You, the Solid Rock, as my foundation. Your presence goes with me, and therefore I am protected as I inherit the land you have for me! I pray blessings on all those people with whom I have had conflicts. Teach me how to love unconditionally as you love. In the name of the Lord Jesus Christ, Amen.

First Things First

Day 4

Let Your Guard Down!

In the church today, there are many people who do not walk daily in a thriving, abundant life with Christ. Though they have accepted Christ as their savior, they are still in bondage in many areas of their lives. They are not experiencing the peace that Jesus offers. On the other hand, there are others who experience God every day, who live a life of freedom, peace and joy, even in the midst of turmoil. They experience genuinely abundant life whether others are around to watch or not. The difference is that some have let God into the most wounded places in their heart to heal and help, while others keep Him on the outer fringes where they limit His ability to work in all areas of their lives.

Sometimes we put a guard around our hearts as a defense mechanism to protect us from harm. This is not necessarily bad. Putting up walls is sometimes good, especially in the midst of a traumatic event. However, many times we allow those walls to remain long after they are needed for protection. The walls then become hindrances that keep God from healing the deepest wounds of our hearts. There comes a time when the walls, originally allowed by God for our survival, need to come down. When the walls stay up, they turn into fortresses of anger, fear and unforgiveness.

There are times when we need well-defined barriers between other people and ourselves. Everyone has weaknesses, and everyone has let someone down. We all have been wounded by someone else's words or actions. Wounded people react to others out of their hurt. As the saying goes, "Hurting people hurt people." If we have healthy barriers in place, we will not succumb to the unrealistic expectations other people try to place on us. We will also not be so hurt when others react to us out of their own hurt.

The problem is when we think that God will be like men. We place the same expectations on God that we place on people. Some people have a hard time getting close to others. They have been controlled and manipulated so many times by people in the past, and they do not want to be run over again. As we realize "God is not a man that He should lie" (Numbers 23:19), we can let down those walls that keep us from an intimate, personal relationship with our Creator.

Not only do we erect walls around our hearts because others hurt us, we also build walls, without even realizing it, when we choose to disobey God. When the Spirit gently woos us to do something and we do not do it, a few more bricks are laid in a wall that will keep us from experiencing God as He wants us to experience Him. The more times we turn from God's call, the more bricks are laid. A bad habit is established. With each choice to disobey Him, the choice to obey Him is harder to make. On the other hand, when we heed His call and do what He stirs our hearts to do, three things will happen:

1. We will experience Him in a way we would not have otherwise.
2. Our faith will increase.
3. It will be easier for us to choose to obey the next time.

Many times the wooing of the Holy Spirit is to simply spend time alone with Him, in His Word, or on our knees. If we heed His call, especially when it means sacrificing something, such as TV or sleep, our relationship with Him will be strengthened in ways we cannot imagine.

When God calls, it is our choice to answer. He will not *make* us do those things He is stirring us to do. Yes, His promptings may be a bit out of our comfort zone. However, the uncomfortable feelings will fade as our obedience gives way to increased faith and joy!

Going Deeper

Imprisoned by our own bars

In Day 3 of the introduction we learned about the walls the enemy places around us to imprison us. Sometimes it is because of our own actions that we have prison bars around us. Read Psalms 107:10-16 and answer the following questions:

Verse 11 – Why are those who are in darkness "bound in affliction and iron" (KJV)?

Verse 12 – Note: God lets us hit the bottom so we will realize our need for Him.

Verse 13 - 14 – What will God do when we finally cry out to Him in our trouble?

Verse 15 – Note: This should lead to thanks and praise to our God!

Verse 16 – What does God do to their gates of brass and bars of iron?

The Wall of Fear

Fear is basically a lack of trust in God. Hanging on to fear will keep a huge barrier around our hearts.

Read 2 Corinthians 7:5-7,

Who wrote this letter? (If you do not know, look at the beginning of the book.)

What does verse 5 say about adverse circumstances Paul had?

Notice that even the Apostle Paul dealt with fear.

In verse 6, how did he say God brought comfort to him?

How else does verse 7 say God brought comfort to Paul?

While God sometimes sends people to demonstrate His love and comfort, some people do not recognize God's help. Those people continue to wallow in their self-pity, complaining that God is not helping them.

God is Not Human!

As we realize that we can trust God and that He is ever faithful and true, we will begin to willingly lower the guards that keep Him from healing our deepest hurts. He is God. He could go behind our walls if He wanted to. But He loves us so much that He does not want to violate our free will. His question to us is simply, "Are you willing to let your guard down?" Before looking up the following scriptures about God's divine faithfulness, pray and ask God to help you to be willing to surrender every thought that has contributed to hardness in your heart toward Him.

I encourage you to read the following scriptures and write in a journal anything that assures you that God is God.

Isaiah 44:6   Isaiah 59:1   James 1:17   1 John 1:5
Isaiah 40:28   Romans 11:33

Our Part

Read 2 Corinthians 10:3-5 and answer the following questions:
Verse 4 - Whose weapons is this talking about?
So, who is supposed to use the weapons?
Verse 5 – Who is supposed to demolish arguments and take captive every thought?

Note that the battle is in our mind. Thoughts contrary to God's Word will strengthen the hardness of our heart that hinders intimacy with God. Thoughts that come from God will strengthen a heart that trusts in Him. With God's help, we can take thoughts captive that do not line up with the Word of God and allow His truths to take their place.

Prayer

Thank you, oh Lord Most High, that You are ever steadfast and true! Please forgive me for the times I have thought of You as a mere man who will let me down. Not only will You not let me down, but

You have only my best interests at heart. Thank You for Jeremiah 29:11: "For I know the thoughts that I think toward you, says the Lord, thoughts of peace and not of evil, to give you a future and a hope." I pray that You will soften my heart toward You and help me to be willing to let my guard down. I want to let go of fear and hold on to trust in You. As I trust in You, I pray that You will show me how to have healthy boundaries between others and myself. I do not want fortresses that will keep me from loving others and allowing them to love to me. I cannot thank You enough that all this is possible through You! What an awesome God You are! Thank you for loving me unconditionally!

First Things First

Day 5

Lift Up Your Heads, Oh Ye Gates!

As we have seen, the enemy wants to put Jericho walls around us, and those he has erected need to come down. And while we often put up our own walls in an effort to protect ourselves, only God knows how to put up the right kind of walls of defense and protection. He wants to rebuild and restore those walls, as the walls around Jerusalem were rebuilt in the book of Nehemiah.

Nehemiah was a Jew held in captivity in the Persian Empire around 444 B.C. Even in captivity, the favor of God was upon Nehemiah, and he rose in rank to become the king's cupbearer. Nehemiah received word that the people who were left in Jerusalem were in despair. The walls around their city were broken down. When he heard this news, he was very sorrowful.

Were the people of Jerusalem in despair because the walls were down, or were the walls broken down because the people were in despair? Probably both. They were in a downward cycle. Their despair led to not tending to the walls, and broken-down walls led to more despair. Some Christians are the same way. In their despair, they forget about the walls of protection that God has placed around them. They forget that God has given His angels charge over them to keep them in all their ways (Psalm 91:11). They forget the principles laid out in His Word that will protect them if they heed them.

God places walls around us not to keep us bound, but to protect us. The principles found in His Word are our boundaries, defining our safety zone. If we live our lives according to His principles, He will guard our hearts and our minds in Christ Jesus (Philippians

4:7). People may think of God's laws as being too strict. They think that if they follow them, they will not have any freedom. Just the opposite is true. It is when they follow God's principles that they *will* have freedom—freedom from the shackles of so many bondages, including addictions, mental and emotional issues, material needs—and freedom from the consequences of sin, including heartbreak, despair, disease and spiritual death. For example, God's Word tells us to not have sexual relations until marriage and to remain faithful to our spouse. If a man and woman follow those principles, they will never have a sexually transmitted disease. They will also not have tormenting thoughts of previous sexual promiscuity while they are in the marriage bed. They will not experience having a child out of wedlock, or a divorce due to infidelity. They can then freely share with their children what godly sexuality is and tell them, from experience, the blessing that obedience to God's principles has been in their lives. A couple who does this truly models for their children how to handle the God-given gift of sexuality in a way that glorifies the Lord and guards the human soul and body.

Unfortunately, more couples than not have allowed those walls of sexual purity to be broken down. Because of that, despair has settled in the core of many families. Thank God those walls can be repaired just as the walls of Jerusalem were repaired in the book of Nehemiah!

There were many obstacles to repairing those walls. First of all, how could Nehemiah help, since he was in captivity far away? Because of the favor God gave him with the king, the king gave him signed and sealed permission letters to go back to Jerusalem to rebuild the walls. The king also sent captains and horsemen of the army to go with him.

While in Jerusalem, Nehemiah was mocked and ridiculed by his enemies, but he declared to them that his God would help him build the walls. He also declared to his enemies that they had no heritage, right, or memorial in Jerusalem. We also need to declare to our enemy, Satan, that he has no place within our walls!

Nehemiah did not rebuild the walls by himself. He gathered together many of the people of Jerusalem to help. Throughout the process, the enemy tried to discourage them. At times they were discouraged, and sometimes they even compromised with the enemy. But in the end, God helped them to complete the project. The Bible tells us that God even turned the curse of the enemy around to a blessing!

Once the walls were rebuilt, the enemy camped outside them, ready to come in when the gates were opened. So does our enemy, and we must not open our gates to him. We observe and take in many things through what we put in our mouths, what we feel with our hands, what we see with our eyes, what we hear with our ears, and what we smell with our nose. We must not open those gates to the enemy to come in and take control.

The Bible encourages us to open our gates to God. Psalm 24:7-8 says, "Lift up your heads, O you gates! And be lifted up, you ever-lasting doors! And the King of glory shall come in. Who is this King of glory? The Lord strong and mighty, the Lord mighty in battle." As we draw near to God and resist Satan, the walls the enemy has placed around us and the walls we have built up around ourselves will fall. God will strengthen the hedge of protection around us. Let us now lift our heads and let the King of Glory come in!

Going Deeper

God Puts a Hedge Around Us

We must remember that God is faithful to protect us from the enemy (2 Thessalonians 3:3).

Read Job 1:7-12.
Verse 7 - This shows us that Satan actually seeks whom he may devour.

Verse 8 – What does this verse say about Job that tells us he was a godly man?

Verse 9-10 - Why could Satan not get to Job?

Verse 11 – Satan told God that if God would put the hedge of protection down, Job would curse God.

Verse 12 – What condition did God place on the permission He gave Satan to get to Job?

Bottom Line: Satan cannot kill us! Whatever God allows in our lives will end up for our good. "And we know that all things work together for good to those who love God, to those who are the called according to His purpose" (Romans 8:28).

Read Psalm 147:12-14. Praise is due to our God, because He strengthens our gates. His blessings are also passed down to our children. What else does this passage say about what He does? (See verse 14.)

God's Walls of Protection

Read the following passages and write what they have to say about how God shields us:

Psalm 3:3 -

Psalm 5:12 -

Psalm 18:30 -

Psalm 18:35 -

Psalm 91:4 -

Psalm 119:114 -

The Body – We Should Encourage One Another to Strengthen the Walls

There are things we can do to make it easier to allow God to take down the wrong walls and build up the right walls of protection around our hearts. Of course, we need to pray and read our Bibles every day, but we also need to fellowship with other believers. It is hard to live a Christian life without going to church.

Read 1 Peter 2:4-6. What does this passage call Christians?
Who is the cornerstone?

Verse 6 says that we will not be confounded. That means we will not be put to shame or dishonored if we trust in Jesus to be the cornerstone of our wall. He is our sure foundation!

Love is a Protection

What an awesome thought, that God's unconditional love is a wall around us. So strong and solid, yet it is more like a warm blanket enveloping us! Whether we realize it or not, we crave love—both from God and from others. As we allow ourselves to let God clothe us in His love, we then learn how to love others.

Read the following scriptures and answer the questions:
1 John 4:18 – What does perfect love do?

1 Peter 4:8 – What else does love do?

1 Corinthians 13:7 in the NIV Bible says that love protects. We must love each other in the body of Christ. We want to help build up walls of protection in other believers' lives, not tear them down!

Read and underline 1 Corinthians 13:4-7. (Try to use the NIV Bible.)

Prayer

Dear Heavenly Father, thank you so much for placing a hedge of protection around me and my family. Please forgive me for the times that I have not allowed You to tear down the wrong walls around my heart and strengthen the right walls. I do not want any wall around me placed by the enemy or myself that leads to a hard heart toward you. Change my heart to be tender toward You and others around me. Thank You for Your Word that serves as protection for my walk with You. Help me to hide Your Word in my heart, so that I might not sin against You (Psalm 119:11). Thank you for Your faithfulness to repair the walls of protection when I do stumble. Lord, I want to receive all that You have for me, therefore, I lift up my head to You and invite You, the King of Glory, to come in!

The Sense of Taste

Oh, taste and see that the Lord is good;
Blessed is the man who trusts in Him!
Psalm 34:8

Day 1

Taste: The Power of the Tongue

In order to survive, we must eat. God made us with a wonderful sense of taste that allows us to enjoy the foods we eat and at the same time helps protect us from taking in something that would cause us harm.

There are four basic tastes: sweet, sour, salty and bitter. (Some new research points to a fifth taste first discovered by the Japanese, "umami," which detects meaty, broth tastes pointing to our need for amino acids.) We crave sweets because of our need for carbohydrates. We crave salty foods because of our need for sodium chloride. We need a balance of the two. This is the reason we often feel a need to eat something salty after having sweets and vice versa. The best thing we can do is not overindulge in either. Not only do we crave foods we like and need, we also reject foods, including those that are too old and taste sour, as well as poisons that taste bitter.

Flavor is the combination of many things including smells, tastes, textures and temperatures. As much as eighty to ninety percent of the flavor of food comes from the scent. Thus, if one cannot smell, the ability to taste is greatly inhibited. This is the reason that food tastes bland to someone who has a stuffy nose.

We detect taste through our taste buds, approximately ten thousand of them located on the tongue, in the back of our mouth and down the throat. A taste bud consists of twenty to one hundred fifty receptor cells, each of which can respond to all of the four basic tastes, but will detect one better than the others. Each receptor cell is connected to a sensory neuron that takes the information to the brain for processing. These receptor cells live for one to two weeks before being replaced by new ones. As we age, we do not detect tastes as easily as when we were younger, because new receptor cells take longer to replace the ones that die.

For years it has been taught that the following areas of the tongue detect certain tastes. Detectors for salty tastes are spread evenly over the whole tongue. The front of the tongue detects sweet tastes. Sour tastes are detected more on the sides of the tongue. The back of the tongue detects bitter tastes.

Some researchers disagree with this concept of a "taste map." They say that all receptor cells can detect any of the tastes. However, if it is true that they will detect one more quickly and easily than the others, it makes sense that those detecting certain tastes more easily might be clustered together in one area of the tongue.

The tongue also helps us chew, swallow and talk. When we chew our food, the tongue helps push food to the back molars, which help crush the food. Saliva glands on the tongue and in the mouth begin to secrete the saliva. The secretion of the saliva starts the digestion process. The tongue then aids in pushing food down the throat as we swallow. Of course, we cannot talk without the use of our tongue.

Looking at the tongue and just how intricate it is, and how many uses it has, reminds us of just how fearfully and wonderfully the Lord made us! We need to pray that we will use our tongues wisely and be cautious about what we put into our bodies. Not only do we need to be careful about what we put into our mouths, but we also need to examine the fruit that comes out in our speech, as Hebrews 13:15 directs: "Therefore by Him let us continually offer the sacrifice of praise to God, that is, the fruit of our lips, giving thanks to His name."

As we do this, it will help to get us to a place where we can receive God's love and be able to "taste and see that He is good" (Psalm

34:8). As we learned earlier in this chapter, flavor is a combination of many things, including smells, tastes, textures and temperatures. This reminds me of the many characteristics of God that await our palates as we embark on this journey of getting to know Him! (See Ephesians 3:18-19.)

Going Deeper

"Taste and See that the Lord is Good!"

Just as someone cannot taste well if his sense of smell is impaired, he also cannot "taste and see that the Lord is good" (Psalm 34:8) until the Spirit breathes life into him! God did this when He created man. Let's look at how God created us:

> "And the Lord God formed man of the dust of the ground, and breathed into his nostrils the breath of life; and man became a living being." Genesis 2:7

What did God do differently when He created man as opposed to when He created other animals?

The Hebrew word for breath is *ruwach.* Sometimes this word is also translated "the Spirit of God." The Holy Spirit is also known as "the Breath of God." When God breathed into man, He gave us a spirit. The spirit is that part of us which communes with God. Adam and Eve could freely commune with God until sin entered the picture.

Read Genesis 3:1-11.
What happened in verse 8?

In verse 11, what did Adam and Eve do to cause them to want to hide from God and not commune with Him?

Read Genesis 2:16-17. God warned Adam that if he ate of the Tree of Knowledge of Good and Evil, he would surely _____.
That day his spirit died, and the natural process of physical death began.

Read John 3:3,5. What did Jesus tell Nicodemus he had to do to enter the Kingdom of Heaven?

When we surrender our lives to Him, we are born again, and our spirit that was dead is alive!

Read 1 Corinthians 2:11-16. Jot down key points that show we can commune with God, read His Word, understand it and finally "taste and see that He is good" if we have the Spirit dwelling in us.

Sweet/Bitter

The front of the tongue detects sweet tastes; the back detects bitter. Some things we taste, such as saccharin, first taste sweet, but as they are swallowed, they taste bitter. Spiritually, there are two things that taste sweet, but produce bitterness in the stomach:

1. **God's words of judgment**

Read Revelation 10:9. Revelation is a book that contains judgments. They are the Words of God, so they were sweet to John. However, they contain judgment so they were bitter in his stomach.

2. **Sin**

"For the lips of an immoral woman drip honey, and her mouth is smoother than oil;

But in the end she is bitter as wormwood, sharp as a two-edged sword." Proverbs 5:3-4

What do these verses say is sweet and bitter?

Read Mark 4:19. What chokes out the Word and keeps it from becoming fruitful?

Read Hebrews 11:24-26 and answer the following questions:

Verse 25 - What was pleasurable that Moses rejected?
How long does that pleasure last?

Verse 26 - What did he choose that was hard to endure, but in the end was a great reward?

Verse 24 - How did Moses do it? By _____

Write out and meditate on the following scriptures:

Romans 6:23 –

Hebrews 11:6 -

Note: You are seeking Him right now! He will reward you!

Read Ephesians 2 to see how, through Christ, we can escape the life of sin and live victoriously through Him! This is good food! You may want to write in a journal the highlights of the chapter or what God is stirring in your heart.

3 functions of the tongue: chew, swallow, speak

I can remember as a young girl not wanting to eat vegetables. I put them in my mouth because I had to. Then I would just keep chewing not wanting to swallow them. My parents encouraged me to swallow, because the nutrients in the vegetables would not help me until I swallowed them!

We have all heard the saying, "You are what you eat." Our goal as Christians is to be Christ-like. John says that Christ is the Word in flesh. We must "eat" the Word if we want to be like Him. Not only do we have to chew, but we must also swallow or it will not do us any good. We chew the Word by studying the Bible, the written Word. We swallow the Word by asking God how the Word we are studying relates to us and by responding in prayer and obedience as

He guides us in living out His Word. After that, the words that we speak from our mouths will start to reflect His character.

Read the second part of Matthew 12:34. What does this verse say about what is in our heart and the words of our mouth?

Prayer

Lord, I want to know You more! I want to "taste and see" that You are good! Help me as I journey with You on this Bible study through the five senses to chew Your Word, swallow Your Word and speak Your Word to others around me.

The Sense of Taste

Day 2

Misuse Hinders Passion for Christ

Whether we live to be nine or ninety-nine, our life here on Earth is a small speck of time compared with eternity. Some people have the attitude that because our lives are "but a vapor" (James 4:14), we need to enjoy them now while we can and "party hearty!" I remember viewing a beer commercial as a child that said, "Go for the gusto!" The message was that you do not know how long you have, so party now while you can. When I was in college, I witnessed about the love of Christ and salvation to a friend who seemed very interested. However, when I asked if she was ready to give her heart and life to God, she said, "I want to, but not now. Maybe I will be ready in a few years. I'm still young, and I want to party!" What she and the majority of society are missing—and endangering themselves by doing so—is this truth: The way we live our lives now will determine how we spend eternity.

It is true that we are not saved by our works. It is only as we accept what Christ did on the cross for us when He shed His blood as a remission for our sins that we truly inherit eternal life with Him in Heaven. When we do, we will want to live for Him more than for ourselves. Some people are living selfishly to feed their own desires, partying and carousing "while the night is young," as they say, and pushing thoughts out of their minds that they could die today. They go on day after day, night after night, feeding the desires of their sense of taste (and, as we will look into in the next unit, feeding the sensations that their sense of touch brings sexually) without stopping to think that a life of pleasure without Christ will cost them eternal life.

Sadly, many in the church are acting the same way as those in the world. Many are drinking, smoking and eating to the point of gluttony. People in the church have different views on this subject. Take drinking alcohol for instance. Some Christians have firm convictions to not drink alcoholic beverages at all, while others insist that it is all right. It is not my intention to debate this issue. I will say, however, that no matter where you stand on the issue of drinking, it is very clear in the Word that drinking to the point of being drunk is sin (Ephesians 5:18). It is also sin to continue to do something that causes another to sin (Romans 14:13).

Growing up in church, I remember wondering why so many thought that alcohol consumption was a sin, yet they bragged about how many desserts they ate at the church's covered dish dinner. The problem of over-eating is getting worse in the United States. (Of course, we do not want to judge, and we need to remember that some are overweight because of medical reasons. God knows and can deal with individuals.) According to a 2004 report by the Center for Disease Control, the percentage of Americans who are considered overweight (those with a body mass index of 25 or more) has risen from 47.7% in the 1970s to 65.2% in 2002. The percentage of those who are considered obese (with a body mass index of 30 or more) has risen from 15% in the 1970s to 31.1% in 2002.[1]

People often turn to food for comfort during times of depression or anxiety. What ends up happening is that the source of happiness ends up causing more depression or anxiety when they step on the scale. In reality, many people are using food to try to fill a void that only God can fill. As I heard one person say, "Am I so miserable that a doughnut will make me feel good?"

On the other end of the spectrum, more and more people, especially young women, are depriving their bodies of food because they are so concerned about getting fat. This type of eating disorder is called anorexia nervosa. Anorexics suffer from very low self-esteem. Many have a need to control something, and the enemy actually makes them comfortable in their hunger. Hunger turns into satisfaction because they have control over something—what they eat.

As we discussed in the last chapter, God made our ability to taste extremely intricate. He *wants* us to enjoy our sense of taste. However, we need to keep a balanced perspective. Our natural tendency as humans is to think of satisfying our fleshly cravings with no thought of what will fill the deep spiritual void that only Jesus can fill. The end result of one who does not turn to God to fulfill his desires is destruction. That person, as Paul says in Philippians 3:19, is one "... whose end is destruction, whose god is their belly, and whose glory is in their shame—who set their mind on earthly things." Many people who have a lifestyle of carousing actually glory in their shame by bragging about their sins.

Our taste desire is very strong, but usually when someone goes to the extreme and sins in this area, there are more reasons than just satisfying that desire. When Adam and Eve ate the fruit that God had forbidden, they were not just trying to get rid of hunger pains. The enemy used the fruit to entice them in the three areas John wrote about in 1 John 2:16: the lust of the flesh, the lust of the eyes and the pride of life. The enemy still uses those same tactics today—often through what we put in our mouths.

A great way to come against the enemy's tactics is to fast. (Of course, for those who have an eating disorder and deprive themselves of food routinely, a fast is not wise.) Sadly, most Christians never fast. Sometimes, in order to be able to "taste and see that the Lord is good" (Psalm 34:8), we need to bypass taste at the physical level. Fasting helps us empty ourselves of all the clutter in our lives that keeps us from hearing from God. Fasting also reminds us of our need for Him.

Some of my most intimate times with God have been during fasts. Yes, the flesh will rear its ugly head with hunger pangs and weakness, but when the hunger pangs come, they remind me of how hungry I am for God. When I feel weak, I am reminded that I can do nothing without God. I have had some people tell me they cannot fast because they get a headache. What they do not realize is that though they do not want a headache, it is a good thing, because it is a sign that the body is ridding itself of toxins, or poisons, in their system. Other signs of detoxification are bad breath and sweating. These symptoms do not mean that we are sick when we are fasting, but that we are being purified. In fact, after a good fast we will feel great—whole in our spirit, soul and body! Many people find that after a fast their sense of taste is more keen and appreciative of even simple flavors.

Some people cannot fast due to health issues. It is highly recommended that a doctor be consulted before beginning a fast. Rather than going on a complete fast, anyone who has medical issues can go on a partial fast. He can think of some food he can medically do without—such as salt, sugar, coffee, chocolate, or any food or drink he tends to crave. Then he can "present his body a living sacrifice unto the Lord" (Romans 12:1).

Dr. Bill Bright, founder of Campus Crusade for Christ, had a tremendous influence on my life in this area. After he died in June of 2003, I heard an interview replayed in which he strongly urged everyone to fast and pray. He said that some years ago he was impressed to go on a 40-day juice fast and that he had done it every year since then. Dr. Bright said, "According to Scripture, personal experience and observation, I am convinced that when God's people fast with a proper Biblical motive—seeking God's face not His hand—with a broken, repentant, and contrite spirit, God will hear from heaven and heal our lives, our churches, our communities, our nation and world."[2]

I encourage everyone reading this book to consider starting a fast during part of the time you are participating in this Bible study. I don't mean fasting because you feel coerced into doing it, or because you will go on a guilt trip if you do not do it. And I am not encouraging a miserable time of starving yourself and hanging your head low. What I'm urging is fasting because you sincerely want to lay down your life and desires, so that God can transform you into what He desires for you. Your desire and passion for the Lord will grow, and you just may have some heavy burdens removed!

Isaiah 58:5-6
"Is it a fast that I have chosen,
A day for a man to afflict his soul?
Is it to bow down his head like a bulrush,
And to spread out sackcloth and ashes?
Would you call this a fast,
And an acceptable day to the Lord?

[6] Is this not the fast that I have chosen:
To loose the bonds of wickedness,
To undo the heavy burdens,
To let the oppressed go free,
And that you break every yoke?"

Going Deeper

Desire

Taste in the physical represents desire/passion in the spiritual. We need to be careful that our physical desires do not lead us the wrong way.

Read James 1:14-15. What are the steps that lead to death?

1.

2.

3.

Misuse of the sense of taste

Our sense of taste is very powerful. Our taste buds are often a bigger threat than peer pressure! Read Proverbs 16:26 and Ecclesiastes 6:7.

"Indeed, because he transgresses by wine, he is a proud man, and he does not stay at home. Because he enlarges his desire as hell, and he is like death, and cannot be satisfied, he gathers to himself all nations and heaps up for himself all peoples." Habakkuk 2:5

Write the part of Habakkuk 2:5 that shows how "transgressing by wine" could cause strife in the home.

Write the part that shows that one like this is the one who puts pressure on his peers.

Read Proverbs 23:21 and tell what happens in this life to the drunkard and the glutton.

Read Isaiah 5:11-14. What consumes the people this passage talks about?

In the second part of verse 12, what is the problem with the parties this is talking about?

What We Don't Have to Taste

God gives us many guidelines in His Word to follow, not because He desires to punish us, but because He wants to protect us. There are rewards for following Him!

Read and underline Jesus' words in John 8:31-32.

Read John 8:51. Here we see the ultimate freedom we will have if we abide in and keep His Word, that we will never taste _____ !

What does 1 Corinthians 15:26 call death?

Read Hebrews 2:9, 14-15. Who tasted death for us?

In your own words, tell how He did that and what He released us from.

Of course we will all die physically if the Lord does not come back first. The death we will not taste is talked about in Rev. 2:11; it is called the _____ death. Read Rev. 21:8 to find out what the second death is.

Fasting

Read Romans 12:1-2. You may not think that this is a passage on fasting, but what better way is there to present our bodies a living sacrifice than to fast? With that in mind, read verse 2 again, and write what can happen to us when we fast.

Read Ezra 8:23. What great thing does this verse say God did for them when they fasted and prayed?

Read and underline 2 Chronicles 7:14.

Fasting is definitely humbling! However, when we fast we do not just need to be humbled; we must use the time to seek His face and turn from our wicked ways. That is when He will hear and answer us and heal our land! Many people, including myself, have used this verse to claim revival for their country. Could it mean He will heal our homes? Could it mean that everywhere your feet go in the "land" where He has divinely appointed, you will be in peace? Grant it, Lord!

Prayer

Father, God, please forgive me for the times I have lived only for my physical desires and passions. Those were the times when I did not seek You. Forgive me for the times I have hurt people in my life while living selfishly with no regard for You or for others. I ask that You help me humble myself to go beyond feeding the cravings of my physical body so that I may look to You to feed the cravings of my spiritual being. Thank You so much for giving me abundant life here on earth. Thank You for keeping me from tasting death, as I will have eternal life with You in Heaven!

The Sense of Taste

Day 3

The Fruit of our Tongue and our Deeds

It makes sense that the part of the body used for taste is also used for speech. The Word says in Proverbs 18:20-21, "A man's stomach shall be satisfied from the fruit of his mouth, from the produce of his lips he shall be filled. Death and life are in the power of the tongue, and those who love it will eat its fruit."

What we put into our bodies is very important. Even more important is what kind of fruit we are producing with our speech. Are our words producing death or life for us and for those who hear them?

When I had laryngitis several years ago, the doctor told me, "If you talk at all in the next couple of days, you could do permanent damage to your vocal chords." That is all he had to say. I took around a pad of paper and stopped talking for three days! (Those who know me will say that in itself is a miracle!) Some people need to hear a similar warning, "If you talk at all in the next couple of days, you could do permanent damage to your relationship." I have seen people in strained relationships that consume their thoughts and words. Whether it is a relationship with a spouse, parent, friend, pastor, boss or coworker, the words that you say to them — or to others about them — will either strengthen or tear down the relationship.

All of us have weaknesses. We all "fall short of the glory of God," according to Romans 3:23. One thing the Lord dealt with me about early in my marriage was to not talk about my husband's weaknesses to other people. Some ladies (and I'm sure some men as well) have a tendency to get together and compare what they do not like about their spouses. The seeds sown with those words will produce fruit that will be harmful to the very foundation of the marriage and home. What starts out as a little joke about something that gets on our nerves about our spouse may end up leading to bigger offenses as the enemy magnifies those things in our mind, even as we speak them.

In the Bible, words are often representative of other things. The Hebrew word picture for "words that come from the mouth" is arrows (Psalm 64:3). We need to realize that the words that come from our mouths are weapons that can either be used for protection against the enemy or for destruction. Thus, the words we say to or about someone can be used for either the protection or for the destruction of our relationship with that person. The problem is that often when we speak, instead of praying first and seeking God on what the truth is about a given situation, we interpret what we think are the facts. We pull back our bows, flippantly shooting those arrows without any thought of aiming toward a target! On the other hand, when someone we are with starts doing that, we need to take cover, because flying arrows are being randomly shot all around us!

How can we be sure that the words coming from our mouths will produce good fruit? One way is by matching our words with God's words! Think about the fruit that His words produce! He spoke the Word and created the heavens and earth! Our words represent arrows, but God's Word is, according to Hebrews 4:12, "sharper than any double-edged sword, it penetrates even to dividing soul and spirit, joints and marrow; it judges the thoughts and attitudes of the heart." God is the only one who sees the whole picture. If we do not know what God has to say about a given situation, maybe we should learn to keep our mouths shut! James 1:19-20 says, "So then, my beloved brethren, let every man be swift to hear, slow to speak, slow to wrath; for the wrath of man does not produce the righteousness of God."

The words we speak will lead to the actions we take. It is a cycle. We conceive a thought and speak what is in our hearts. Then we carry out what started in our hearts through our actions (both good and bad). Those actions then strengthen the original seeds of thought that produced them, and growth occurs.

What are we allowing to grow in our hearts and lives? It could be a strong, fruit-bearing tree, or it could be weeds. We need to cultivate the trees and pull the weeds out by the roots before they get too big. Right after my husband and I moved into our house many years ago, we noticed a particular weed that kept growing at the edge of our back yard. I remember talking about how we needed to get out there and pull the weed. Well, we did not, and the weed ended up being a tree—a non-fruit-bearing tree!

Let us first look at this in a positive light. When someone invites Jesus into his heart and life to be his Savior and Lord, he thinks of Him often. He thinks of the peace and joy that only God can bring and of His goodness that brought forgiveness. He speaks of Him to others. Whether the person to whom he witnesses responds to God's love or not, the young Christian's faith grows stronger each time he shares his faith. The fruit tree grows! If he continues to allow that tree to be cultivated, and if he allows God to do regular weeding around the tree, the tree will grow! As Psalm 1:3 says, "He shall be like a tree planted by the rivers of water, that brings forth its fruit in its season, whose leaf also shall not wither; and whatever he does shall prosper."

In "Going Deeper" of the last chapter we looked at how the desires to fulfill our sense of taste can hinder our passion for Christ. James 1:14-15 says, "But each one is tempted when he is drawn away by his own desires and enticed. Then, when desire has conceived, it gives birth to sin; and sin, when it is full-grown, brings forth death." That does not sound like good fruit to me! Let's break it down.

According to verse 14, our desires are the reason we are tempted: "But each one is tempted when he is drawn away by his own desires and enticed." If we did not have a desire for something, it would not even be a temptation. What a joy it is when we realize that we have allowed God to change our desires. What once was a stumbling block is not even a temptation anymore!

It is important to know, however, that temptation itself is not a sin. As long as we are living we will experience temptations. We are told in 1 Corinthians 10:13 that temptation is "common to man." The good news is that with every temptation God has allowed a "way of escape." So, depending on how we choose to react to the temptation, we will either end up carrying out the temptation and sinning, or we will escape victoriously!

Verse 15 of James 1 warns us what will happen if we do not take the high road and choose the way of escape that God so faithfully provides. Again, it says, "When desire has conceived, it gives birth to sin; and sin, when it is full-grown, brings forth death." It is a downward spiral. Our desires allow us to be tempted. When we follow through with the temptation to sin, we chip away at our set of standards and sin again, and again, and again. This leads to death— death of a dream, death of a relationship, death of joy and peace— the list goes on and on. We must remember that God is faithful. He can stop the downward spiral if we let Him! We must look to Him! As we do, He will reveal the lies of the enemy to which we have been clinging and replace those lies with His truth. As we choose to spend quality time getting to know Him intimately, our desires will change to become His desires. We will look back and see how He stopped the downward spiral in our lives and replaced it with an upward spiral of an overcoming life!

Romans 6:16-22:

"Don't you know that when you offer yourselves to someone to obey him as slaves, you are slaves to the one whom you obey—whether you are slaves to sin, which leads to death, or to obedience, which leads to righteousness? [17] But thanks be to God that, though you used to be slaves to sin, you wholeheartedly obeyed the form of teaching to which you were entrusted. [18] You have been set free from sin and have become slaves to righteousness.

[19] I put this in human terms because you are weak in your natural selves. Just as you used to offer the parts of your body in slavery to impurity and to ever-increasing wickedness, so now offer them in slavery to righteousness leading to holiness. [20] When you were slaves to sin, you were free from the control

of righteousness. [21] What benefit did you reap at that time from the things you are now ashamed of? Those things result in death! [22] But now that you have been set free from sin and have become slaves to God, the benefit you reap leads to holiness, and the result is eternal life."

Going Deeper

Fruit of our words and deeds

Jesus likens our words to fruit. Read Matthew 12:33-37 and write in your own words what this is saying about fruit and words that we speak.

Read the following scriptures on the fruit of our words and deeds. You may want to write in a journal any scripture that stirs your heart and your responses or prayers.

Proverbs 12:14   Proverbs 12:18   Proverbs 18:20
Isaiah 3:10   Jeremiah 17:10   Hebrews 13:15

Hold Fast Your Confession; Escape Temptation

Read Hebrews 4:14-16.

Verse 14 - The Greek word for "confession" is *homologia. Homo* means "same." *Logia* means "word." We "hold fast our confession" by matching our words with God's words.

Verse 15 - Jesus can sympathize with our weaknesses. He was fully human, and He was tempted, yet He was without sin. You may want to read Matthew 4 about the temptation of Christ. Related to our topic of taste, the first temptation was about eating. Satan knew Jesus had just fasted for 40 days and would be hungry. Satan knows our areas of weaknesses, and that is where he comes to tempt us. We need to do as Jesus did and respond to the enemy with God's Word, "It is written ...!"

Verse 16 - Because of Jesus, how can we now approach the throne of grace in the time of need?
Why? Because He is faithful!!

Read and underline Hebrews 10:23.

Yet another reminder of His faithfulness to help us in the time of temptation:

> "No temptation has overtaken you except such as is common to man; but God is faithful, who will not allow you to be tempted beyond what you are able, but with the temptation will also make the way of escape, that you may be able to bear it." 1 Corinthians 10:13

Developing the Fruit of the Spirit
Read Galatians 5:19-26 and list any "works of the flesh" that you especially want God to help you overcome.

Write out a prayer concerning those works of the flesh. You may want to include repentance, a cry for divine help in overcoming, a declaration of resisting the enemy, thanksgiving to God for seeing you through, etc.

Notice that good works are not listed in the fruit of the Spirit. We need to get off the performance treadmill and seek God to develop genuine fruit in our lives. List any fruit of the Spirit that you feel especially stirred to have developed at this time in your life.

Write out a prayer concerning this.

You may want to get a notebook and do your own Bible study on one or more of the fruits of the Spirit. Get a concordance or a study Bible and do your own scripture search!

How is fruit developed? Read John 15:4-5. What is the only way we will bear fruit?

What can we do without God?

We need to focus on abiding, not on doing! The Greek word for abide is *meno*. According to the Strong's Concordance, it means to stay in a given place, state, relation or expectancy: abide, continue, dwell, endure, be present, remain, stand, tarry.[1]

Read Psalm 91. The Hebrew word for dwell here is *yashab*. It is very similar to the Greek word for abide. However, it also carries a meaning of "settling down."[2] Sometimes we need to learn how to settle down and not conform to the business of the world around us. Only then will we learn how to "abide in the vine" and "dwell in the secret place of the Most High."

Earlier we read about taking cover when someone else begins randomly shooting his arrows (words). Now we know that it is scriptural to do that! Psalm 91 gives a list of the things that will not hurt you if you "dwell in the secret place of the Most High." Which verse in Psalm 91 states that the "arrows that fly by day" (or the words that people say!) will not hurt you?

List other things Psalm 91 tells us will happen if we learn to dwell in the Lord:

Prayer

Lord, my prayer today comes from Your Word in Philippians 1:9-11. I pray that my love would abound still more and more in knowledge and all discernment, and that I might approve the things that are excellent. I pray that I would be sincere and without offense till the day of Christ, and that I may be filled with the fruit of righteousness. Lord Jesus, please remind me to let the fruit of righteousness come out in my words and in how I treat others, so that they may eat of the fruit and be drawn to You, the giver of that fruit unto the glory of God! Thank you so much for taking on humanity and enduring temptation so that I may come to Your throne boldly in my time of need! Your faithfulness endures throughout all generations! Amen!

The Sense of Taste

Day 4

Eat the Word; Drink in the Spirit

H aving grown up in the church, I have heard many discussions about when to have personal devotions or quiet time with the Lord. Actually, the first step is simply to have a quiet time. Many people are fasting spiritual food instead of physical food. Some Christians are like starving children in foreign lands. They are living, but very malnourished. Spiritually speaking, they have been born—yes, they gave their heart to the Lord years ago—but their limbs are like bare bones, and their bellies are swollen. They even have flies swarming around and they will not do anything to shoo them away. Why? They will not eat! It is not because spiritual food is not available; it is that they just will not eat.

Not only are there Christians who are spiritually anorexic because they choose not to eat, but there are also Christians in the other extreme who are very spiritually obese. Especially in America, there is plenty spiritual food to eat. It is like going to an all-you-can-eat buffet. They go to the all-you-can-eat spreads as often as they can. The problem is, they eat too much of the wrong kinds of food, and not enough natural, healthy foods. They also take in, take in, take in until they are so stuffed they can barely walk out of the restaurant. Then, they do not exercise. They cannot continue to take in and not exert energy to burn off the calories, or they will just put on more weight.

Oh yes, in America, we've got a spread that won't quit: drinks, bread, salads, appetizers, vegetables, entrees and an assortment of desserts that start the saliva glands flowing! We've got Christian

71

radio; churches on nearly every corner, or at least within a few miles of one another; Christian book stores with books, tapes and worship CDs; websites and emails with daily thoughts, how-tos and more; conferences, retreats and seminars—the list goes on and on! I will say that I do love all those things. However, sometimes we need to pull back and "fast" some of those things so that we can do what Jesus did when He so often pulled away from crowds to get alone with God the Father.

Books on prayer are good, but they do not help us if we do not close the book at some point and actually put those principles into action and pray! Commentaries and Christian living books are good, but sometimes we need to put down the book about someone else's interpretation of God's Word and go directly to God's Word. 2 Peter 1:3 says that God "has given us all things that pertain to life and godliness, through the *knowledge of Him* that has called us to glory and virtue." (Emphasis is mine.)

What would happen if suddenly there were a ban in America on all Christian radio and TV and all the Christian bookstores had to close? That day very well might come. We found out just how suddenly a terrorist attack could cripple us on 9-11-01 when suicide "martyrs" took airplanes—commercial jet airplanes full of innocent people—and crashed them into both towers of the World Trade Center in New York and into the Pentagon in Washington. We saw seemingly indestructible fortresses crumble to the ground like a child's tower of blocks. Who knows what havoc would have been wrought by the plane that ended up in a field if some true, unselfish heroes had not acted as they did.

Yes, it could happen suddenly. The all-you-can-eat establishments could be totally shut down. It might be worse if it all happens gradually. That is what I feel is happening in America, even as I write this. Many in the church are like frogs in a kettle. As the heat gradually gets turned up, the frog's body temperature changes with it so the frog is comfortable until finally the frog boils with the water and dies. Wake up, church! It does not matter what the 1st Amendment says; it only takes one ungodly, immoral judge to interpret a law his or her own way to start changing the very Judeo-Christian fabric upon which this nation was founded.

It just might happen. We may not have access to Bible studies like this in the future. What are we going to do? What if we did not have access to Bibles? Do we have enough memorized to get us by? There are people in foreign lands right now who are experiencing that very thing. They are starving for the Word. There are underground churches where believers thrill to get their hands on just a few pages of the Bible. They swarm around it, pass it around, and memorize it so they can take it with them. Though the Ten Commandments have been banned from courthouses in America, no ungodly, immoral judge can take the Ten Commandments out of our hearts!

As to the question, "When should I have my quiet time, in the morning or evening?" the answer is "YES!" Psalm 92:1-2 says, "It is good to give thanks to the Lord, and to sing praises to Your name, O Most High; to declare Your lovingkindness *in the morning*, and Your faithfulness *every night.*" (Emphasis added.)

We need to give God the first fruits of our time by rising earlier than usual so that we can spend time with Him. Then we can take the time to thank Him that His mercies are new every morning and to seek Him and place our agenda for the day in His hands to guide us as He sees fit. We also need to set aside time with Him before we lay our heads to rest at night to recount the ways He was faithful to us that day. Then we can lay everything that happened at His feet. I am not saying how much time we need to give Him. What I am saying is, if we start our day right and end it right with the only righteous One—our Creator—then it does not matter how the day went, He will get us back on track. The divine purposes He has in store for our lives will be accomplished.

An email (from an unknown source) that was forwarded to me is an illustration of how, if we start right and end right, things will work out, even if the in-between does not go so well. Here is what the email said:

Aoccdrnig to rscheearch at Cmabrigde Uinervtisy, it deosn't mttaer what oredr the ltteers are in a wrod, the olny ioptmrant tnihg is taht the frist and lsat ltteer be at the rghit pclae. The rset can be a ttaol mses and you can sitll raed it wouthit

73

a porbelm. Tihs is bcuseae the huamn mnid deos not raed ervey lteter by iletsf, but the wrod as a wlohe. Naet huh?

I venture to say that as we give the first of our day and the last of our day to the Lord, we will notice that He will teach us how to be aware of His presence all day long. We will then begin to know what it means to live a life in which we "pray without ceasing" (1 Thessalonians 5:17).

Going Deeper

Marriage of the Word and the Spirit
God is calling us to be a church that emphasizes being grounded in the Word of God *and* empowered by the Holy Spirit. It is important not to emphasize one over the other. Some churches emphasize the preaching and teaching of the Word, and encourage their people to have a personal time of Bible study, but they are afraid of any move of the Spirit. Other churches emphasize being empowered by the Holy Spirit, determined not to be bound by any programs or schedules of services, and they sometimes miss out on solid Biblical teaching. The first type of church is afraid of losing control, and the latter is afraid of control and manipulation. God cannot be put in a box either way! We need to seek Him, and let Him guide us into the Word and fellowship of the Spirit. The church that has this balance of the Word and the Spirit will see people in their congregations being stirred by the Spirit with specific passions to be used of God. They will have the solid foundation of the Word needed to carry out the call of God. Oh, yes! Here comes the latter rain!!

Scriptures on being grounded in the Word:

Read the following verses and answer the questions:
Hebrews 4:12 - What does this verse say about the Word?

John 17:17 – Write what Jesus prayed to the Father.

To sanctify is to make holy. Do you want to live a holy life unto the Lord? Bible study is imperative!

2 Tim. 3:15 - 16 - What are the scriptures that many of us have been taught since childhood able to do for us?

"All Scripture is given by inspiration of God, and is profitable for doctrine, for reproof, for correction, for instruction in righteousness" (2 Tim. 3:16). List the four things for which verse 16 says the Word is "profitable" to help us live an overcoming life:

1. _____ - lets us know right and wrong

2. _____ - means to express disapproval of, reminds us to leave the sin

3. _____ - gets us back on track

4. _____ - preventative maintenance

Psalm 19:7 - The law of the Lord (His Word) is _____. What does it do?

Scriptures on the Holy Spirit:
Read the following verses and answer the questions:
John 14:26 – What is the Holy Spirit called?
What will He do?

Mark 1:8 - What did John the Baptist say in this verse about Jesus?

Acts 1:4-8 - These are the words of Jesus before He ascended into Heaven and are a fulfillment of what John the Baptist said in Mark 1:8. According to verse 8, what will you receive when the Holy Spirit comes upon you?

Then you will be _____. (Acts 2 records what happened on the Day of Pentecost when this promise was first fulfilled.)

Romans 8:14-16 – What does this passage say about those who are led by the Spirit?

It is by the Spirit that we *know* we are God's children!

1 Corinthians 12:4-11 – According to verse 7, why are these gifts of the Holy Spirit given?

Who decides how the gifts are distributed?

Remember, these are His gifts, not ours. He uses us as His vessel to give gifts to others.

2 Corinthians 3:17-18 – What does verse 17 say about where the Spirit of the Lord is?

What does verse 18 say about what is happening to us by the Spirit?

The Word - the Bread of Life
Read John 6:31-34 and John 6:48-51. Compare manna and Jesus, the Bread of Life:

In John 1, Jesus is called "The Word." Jesus is the Word in flesh. The Bible is the written Word. We need the Word daily, just as the Israelites needed the manna daily. We would not think of going without natural food each day (with the exception of when we are fasting). Neither should we go without spiritual food from the Bible.

The Spirit - the Living Water

Read the following verses and answer the questions:
John 4:10-14 - Who gives living water?

John 7:38-39 - According to verse 38, from where does Jesus say this "living water" will flow?
According to verse 39, what is the "living water" referring to?

1 Corinthians 3:16 – What does this verse call us?

The temple was divided into sections: the outer courts, the inner courts, the Holy Place, and the Most Holy of Holies where the Ark of the Covenant with God's manifest presence was kept. Before Jesus was crucified, only the High Priests could enter the Holy of Holies. Mark 15:38 tells us that when Jesus died on the cross, the veil that separated the Holy of Holies from the Holy Place was torn in two from the top to the bottom. The Greek word for temple in 1 Corinthians 3:16 is *naos*. It is the same word used for the Holy of Holies! The presence of God dwells in us!!

2 Corinthians 13:14 - This is a scripture pointing to the triune God. It talks of the _____ of the Holy Spirit. Just as we need "daily Bread" from Bible study, it is very important that we have daily communion with the Holy Spirit. This relationship comes when we truly desire to spend time in worship.

Read and underline John 4:24.

Prayer

Dear Lord, help me to be hungry for You! Please give me a desire to read Your Word and fellowship with You. I pray that You will guide me in setting my priorities. Help me to have more time alone to spend reading Your Word and worshipping You. Thank You, Holy Spirit for revealing to me the truths in Your Word as I read it. Thank You for reminding me in my thoughts of scriptures I need throughout the day. Help me respond to Your love as I spend time with You. Thank You that "in Your presence is fullness of joy" (Psalm 16:11) and that I can be in Your presence even as I go about my daily routine. I want to eat of Your Word and drink in Your Spirit every day of my life!

The Sense of Taste

Day 5

Desire and Passion for the Lord

Our sense of taste is fueled by our desire to satisfy our hunger and thirst. Once we experience foods and drinks that are pleasing to our taste buds, our desire turns into a passion for specific foods and drinks. No longer are we satisfied with just any food or drink, but we do what we can to find those flavors that we enjoy. People will drive across town to go to a restaurant they love, while passing dozens of restaurants and grocery stores along the way. (In the same way, people will pass many churches as they drive across town to a church that feeds them God's Word and where they can drink in His Spirit!)

Sometimes our passions can consume us and lead to a downward spiral of addiction. Dieting and eating what is healthy is difficult when the array of tasty foods that are filled with fats and sugars are so plenteous. I have found, however, that when I make a point of choosing naturally healthy foods, and drinking more water for a period of days, I feel so much better. Not only that, but my body starts craving the good things. When I go back and eat salty snacks or desserts, I eat them in moderation, because they now taste too salty and too sweet! I used to not drink much water at all. I read articles and saw health reports on TV about how drinking water promotes good health in many different ways, but I just did not have a desire for water. Once I started making myself drink water, even if I didn't like tasting something without any sweetness or flavor, my body started craving it. I now like to take a water bottle with me wherever

I go, so I can satisfy that thirst I never knew I had before! Nothing satisfies the thirst like pure, unadulterated water!

Likewise, sometimes we just have to open the Bible and read it, whether we desire to or not. God said His Word would not return void. The Bible is not like any other book. It is living and powerful! (See Hebrews 4:12.) It promotes health in the body, soul and spirit (Proverbs. 4:20-22). Once we experience the difference the Word, illuminated by the Spirit, makes in our lives, we will start craving it. We will be aware of a hunger we never knew we had. It is an addiction that God wants us to have! In fact, He invites us to have it.

"Ho! Everyone who thirsts,
Come to the waters;
And you who have no money,
Come, buy and eat.
Yes, come, buy wine and milk
Without money and without price.
[2] Why do you spend money for what is not bread,
And your wages for what does not satisfy?
Listen carefully to Me, and eat what is good,
And let your soul delight itself in abundance." Isaiah 55:1-2

Yes, sometimes we just need to read the Bible whether we desire it or not, and our desires will start changing to want more of the Word. On the other hand, I have also found that if we pray and ask God for a desire for more of His Word, He will give it to us. Actually, we already have that desire, because He created all of us with a void that can only be filled by Him! He then takes off the clutter, little by little, that has been dumped on top of that innate desire to get to know Him. As we spend more time with Him, sometimes on our faces before Him, seeking Him and not asking for things, our desires start changing, conforming to His desires. We will make it our aim to please Him. It is then that John 15:7 can happen in our lives! It says, "If you abide in Me, and My words abide in you, you will ask what you desire, and it shall be done for you."

As we seek God and allow His words to abide in us, a passion for Christ will burn like a fire within us. As with any fire, we must add more fuel or wood to keep the flame burning. How do we do that? First, we need to let the Lord show us the lies of the enemy that we hang onto that hinder our passion, and replace them with His truth. Then we must remember to read our Bibles and pray every day as well as get involved in a good church where we can be discipled and have much-needed fellowship with other believers.

The enemy's first tactic to keep us from having passion for Christ is isolation. He will throw a thought bomb in our heads that says, "You don't need to go to church to be a Christian." If we listen to that, we will miss church every once in a while when we "accidentally sleep in." Then we will get out of the habit of going. Finally we will be like a single little coal that is removed from the fire and eventually goes out. We will lack the passion for Christ that brings abundant life to us and those around us. That was the enemy's plan all along—to keep us from having a passion for Christ.

To be effective in anything we do, we must have passion. For a short time in my life, I was a consultant for a direct sales organization. I remember going to the annual convention, sitting back and observing how much they were trying to motivate us to have a passion for their product. I sat there and thought how the same principles they were applying could be effective in God's Kingdom. Here is what I learned:

1. Have a passion for your product.
2. Have information about the product everywhere you go, mentioning it to your family, friends, cashiers, waitresses, Little-League moms, neighbors, etc.
3. Offer it to everyone. Why? Everyone deserves the opportunity you have! If you offer it to Sue and Sally, but skip Debbie because you think she's not interested, Debbie might be offended.

There were some at the convention who were only consultants so they could get the product at cost. They would not promote their business, because they did not want to pressure anyone. They did get the product at cost, but their business would never advance. Without promoting their product with passion they would not have any recruits, and they would never receive any of the bonuses offered for high achievement.

In the same way, some Christians are just Christians to avoid going to hell. They do not want to "push their beliefs" on anyone. Yes, they may miss hell, but they will never know what a spiritual high they can have by merely sharing their faith. They will also miss out on rich blessings in store for them, and they will not have any "recruits" to take with them to Heaven. In effect, because they are not storing up any treasure in Heaven (Matthew 6:20), and they are not reaping the benefits of a Spirit-filled, evangelizing life on earth, their lives on either side of the grave are not what they could be. How sad!

Why do many Christians lack a passion to promote Christ to those around them? The bottom line is that they are focused on self. They might say it is because they are timid. They might be embarrassed to promote Christ because of how they will look, caring more about what people think than about what God thinks. Either way, it is pride. The center of pride is "I," which is also the center of SIN — Self-Indulgent Nature. This self-centeredness is what propels addictions and hinders spiritual hunger. The answer then is to "die to self" and place ourselves on the altar. This is an ongoing process. Someone once said, "The sacrifice keeps crawling off the altar!" That's why Paul said, "I die daily" (1 Corinthians 15:31).

Do you want a fire of passion for Christ to burn within you? What you need is an intimate relationship with Him! Those who have experienced intimacy with God cannot help but share Him with those around them. Ask God for the desire to get to know Him intimately. The Bible says that we have not, because we ask not (James 4:2).

Oh, friend! It is time to have a passion for Christ! I urge you to seek God for a passion. Read His Word. Spend time alone with Him. Let Him keep the flame burning within your spirit.

Going Deeper

Affection

Another word for *passion* is *affection*. You will be affected by what you focus your affections on, whether good or bad. There is no staying the same. What do you want to affect you?

Read Colossians 3:1-5. What is Paul telling us to do in these verses?

Verse 3 is a reminder to "die to self" and fleshly desires. Write out a prayer to God in response to Colossians 3:1-5.

Suffering

Another translation for the Greek word for *passion* is *suffering*. In Acts 1:3 the NIV Bible speaks of Jesus' suffering. The KJV Bible translates it passion. Everyone knows that a passion play is about Christ's sufferings. He had to have passion for us, or He would not have gone through all that suffering for us.
Read Hebrews 12:1-3 and answer the following questions:
What does verse 1 tell us to do?

Verse 2 tells us how. We have to look to _____.
Why did He endure the cross?

When someone lies about you or mistreats you, what should you do according to verse 3?

Read and underline Philippians 2:7-8.

Read Hebrews 2:9. What did Jesus do for everyone?

In Hebrews 5:7-8, the author tells of the level of suffering Christ experienced by saying He offered up prayer with _____

_____.

(We know that this was when He was praying in the Garden of Gethsemane before He was taken to be crucified. Luke 22:44 says that as He was praying in agony, His sweat was like great drops of blood.)

According to verse 8, what did Jesus learn through suffering?

Read 1 Peter 2:21-23.
Verse 21 says, "Christ, who suffered for us, left us an _____
that we should _____."

Verse 23 shows us the example Christ was for us when He suffered. What does this say He did that we should also do when we are falsely accused, misunderstood and mistreated?

Philippians 3:10:

"… that I may know Him and the power of His resurrection, and the fellowship of His suffering, being conformed to His death…"

In the verse above, underline the words, "know" and "suffering." Do you want to know Him? You have to be willing to share in His sufferings. The Greek word for *know* here is *ginosko*. It means to know and understand. According to Vine's *Expository Dictionary of New Testament Words*[1], "In the N.T. *ginosko* frequently indicates a relationship between the person knowing and the object known; in this respect, what is known is of value or importance to the one who knows, and hence the establishment of the relationship." This points to a relationship with Christ, not merely knowing about Him.

Ginosko is also the word used for the union of man and wife sexually, the most intimate "knowing" two people can have (Genesis 4:1).

Read 1 Peter 4:1. Suffering for Christ helps us overcome sinful desires. Write out the last part of this verse.

Good news!!! According to 2 Corinthians 1:5, if we are in Christ, what is just as sure as our suffering?

Psalm 34:18 (NIV) "The Lord is close to the brokenhearted and saves those who are crushed in spirit."

Read and meditate on the whole of Psalm 34. You may want to write in your journal the things from this Psalm that the Lord stirs in your spirit to be able to "taste and see that the Lord is good" (Psalm 34:8).

Prayer

Lord, I am hungry for You! Help me to count the cost and be willing to do whatever it takes to know you more intimately, even if it means I have to suffer for You. Thank You that You will be with me through whatever I go through, and that on the other side of each trial, the joy of experiencing You will be far greater than anything I have to go through. Thank You for enduring the cross for me!

The Sense of Touch

*"Wherever He entered into villages, cities, or in the
country, they laid the sick in the marketplaces, and begged
Him that they might just touch the hem of His garment. And
as many as touched Him were made well." Mark 6:56*

Day 1

Touch: More than Skin Deep

Of all the senses in the human body, the sense of touch seems to be the one that affects the whole being—spirit, soul and body—more than any other sense. When a crying baby feels the warmth and comfort of a mother's arms, he is calmed and contented. The soothing touch of a massage therapist not only releases tension in tight muscles, but it also helps to release toxins from our body and lessens stress from our emotions. A simple kiss will arouse romantic feelings between a man and a woman.

Not only does touch affect the whole body, but the main organ that is used to experience touch, the skin, is visibly affected by stimuli that enter through all the senses as well as by thoughts and emotions. Think about it: You may have experienced this both in a negative and a positive way. If someone comes to you in a fit of rage and confronts you with accusations you were not expecting, a cold sweat may come over you. On the other hand, if you hear a testimony of how God worked in great and small details of someone's life, or if you experience Him intimately yourself, goose bumps may form on your skin.

Touch is the only sense that we experience all over our body, because skin covers the entire body. In fact, in an average adult, the skin accounts for about sixteen percent of total body weight. There are nerve endings or receptors throughout the skin that carry information to the brain about the things we touch, and that touch us. The brain then registers what we feel, such as temperature, pressure, texture and pain.

Our skin has layers. The bottom layer, the dermis, is where the blood vessels, hair follicles, oil glands, nerve endings and sweat glands are located. The sweat glands excrete waste, regulate our body temperature and moisten our skin. They are especially sensitive to stimuli we receive from other senses and our nervous system. This is why some people sweat when they eat too much spicy food. It is also why someone might begin to sweat if he hears very disturbing news.

The epidermis is above the dermis and is composed of many layers. Because it is largely impermeable to water, it keeps essential fluids in the body, and it keeps fluids that might contain something harmful to us from entering the body. By the time the skin cells reach the top of the epidermis they are dead, and new skin cells are replenishing the layers just below the surface. In fact, the epidermis is renewed every fifteen to thirty days.

Within the epidermis are cells that produce the pigment melanin. This pigment determines the color of the skin. Every human's skin color is produced by the same thing: melanin. Some people just have more than others, so they are darker. It is the melanin that protects us from the harmful ultraviolet rays of the sun.

There are other types of skin cells in our body, such as those that give it durability and elasticity. Another kind of cell protects us from injury or illness and works to destroy any substance these cells identify as foreign or dangerous to the body. God made us so intricately that our body, when functioning properly, works to heal itself!

Research has shown that touching can actually promote healing. Infants who are born prematurely will progress better if they are held and rocked. In their book, *The Gift of the Blessing*, authors Gary Smalley and John Trent speak of this:

"Interestingly enough, the act of laying on of hands has become the focus of a great deal of modern-day interest and research. Dr. Dolores Krieger, professor of nursing at New York University, has made numerous studies on the effects of laying on of hands. What she found is that both the toucher and the one being touched received a physiological benefit. How is that possible?

Inside our bodies is hemoglobin, the pigment of the red blood cells, which carries oxygen to the tissues. Repeatedly, Dr. Krieger has found that hemoglobin levels in both people's blood streams go up during the act of laying on of hands. As hemoglobin levels are invigorated, body tissues received more oxygen. This increase of oxygen energizes a person and can even aid in the regeneration process if he or she is willing."[1]

What an awesome phenomenon this gift of touch is! The skin, with all its receptors, glands and different types of cells, acts as a barrier between us and the outside world, yet it also helps us to function in our surroundings. And the fact that a meaningful touch from one person to another brings about positive results in both people shows us that we need each other.

Recently, on a Christian radio talk show, the host asked the guest what God meant to him. His response was, "He's as close to me as my skin!" Wow! I thought of how God can be like our skin if we let Him. He will protect us from the outside world with His divine covering, yet He will give us wisdom about how to live in the world. He keeps the water of the Holy Spirit in and instructs us in how to keep harmful influences out. He allows us to feel pain in order to let us know when something needs our attention, when we are in error or in danger, yet He brings about healing, restoring our spirits, minds and bodies! Praise Him that He can be as close as our skin!

Going Deeper

We touch each other in many ways.

According to 1 Peter 2:5, we are called _____.

In a stone building, how close are the stones to each other?

Notice that unlike bricks, stones are each uniquely shaped. They fit in just the right place. Like stones in a building, God places each of us in place in the body of Christ right where we fit best. We "touch" each other in ways beyond the physical touch. When we do, we encourage each other and sometimes "sharpen" each other as iron sharpens iron (Proberbs 27:17).

Blessing with a touch

In Bible times, the laying on of hands often represented the consecration and setting apart of one for service. Read Numbers 27:18-21. On whom did the Lord tell Moses to lay his hands in an act of consecration for service?

Fathers also laid their hands on children and blessed them. Read the account of Jacob blessing his grandsons in Genesis 48:8-16. Which verse shows that Jacob kissed them and embraced them?

Jesus also took time out to touch and bless children in Matthew 19:13-15. We need to take time to hug our children and proclaim blessings over them! Appropriate touch in a child's life brings much-needed security.

There's no Room for Prejudice in God's Kingdom!

"For you are all sons of God through faith in Christ Jesus. [27] For as many of you as were baptized into Christ have put on Christ. [28] There is neither Jew nor Greek, there is neither slave nor free, there is neither male nor female; for you are all one in Christ Jesus. [29] And if you are Christ's, then you are Abraham's seed, and heirs according to the promise." Galatians 3:26-29

After reading this passage, what are your thoughts about prejudice?

The walls of prejudice have to come down! Read Ephesians 2:14-18. This passage speaks of the wall of separation between Jews and Gentiles, but it can also pertain to any two groups of people who have animosity toward each other.

Who does this passage say breaks down the wall?

It says that "He is our _____." Peace will never happen anywhere in the world without Jesus in the center! After reading this passage, put in your own words how and why Jesus broke down the wall of separation.

Pause and take some time to pray for the walls to fall and peace through Jesus to come in to your family, church and community. You may be led of the Lord to pray for peace in foreign lands. We especially need to pray for the peace of Jerusalem (Psalm 122:6).

He's as close as our skin!
Just like the skin over our entire body keeps the much-needed water in, so God "seals" us and gives us the Spirit, "living water." Read and underline 2 Corinthians 1:21-22.

He will protect us from the enemy!

2 Thessalonians 3:3 (NIV) "But the Lord is faithful, and he will strengthen and protect you from the evil one." The Greek word for "protect" is phulassoo, which means to protect; to keep; to guard; to defend; to preserve; to cover; to insulate; to safeguard.[2]

Is there a situation you are in right now for which you need His strength and protection?

What part of the definition for "protect" brings you comfort and why?

"But may the God of all grace, who called us to His eternal glory by Christ Jesus, after you have suffered a while, perfect, establish, strengthen, and settle you." 1 Peter 5:10

Just as sweat brings balance to us by getting rid of waste, regulating our body temperature, and moistening our skin, so God does that when He "establishes" us. Besides establishing us, what other words does Peter use to describe what God does for us in 1 Peter 5:10?

Notice it says He will do this after we _____.

Remember that sometimes pain is necessary, but God brings healing!

He will bring healing to our wounds!

Read and underline Psalm 147:3.

Read Luke 4:18 and write a prayer of response to what you read.

Prayer

Oh, Lord, You are so amazing!! Thank You for placing people in my life who will bring a healing touch to me. Thank You also for using me in the lives of others to bring a healing touch. Thank You that You cover each of us who are in Christ Jesus, just as the skin on our body covers us. You are our protection. You are our seal. You are our refuge. You establish us and bring us balance. You bring us healing. What more could we ever ask for? May my praise and awe of You even now touch You and bless You, for You are worthy of our praise!

The Sense of Touch

Day 2

Misuse Hinders Worship

We have seen how beautifully God created us with the ability to touch and feel. Only God could so intricately make us! He has given us this remarkable sense that allows us to experience pleasure for our enjoyment (as well as pain as a warning to stay away from things that will harm us).

One of the most special experiences we can have through the sense of touch is the gift of sex between a husband and wife. In fact, it is so special that God uses it as an illustration of Christ and the church (Ephesians 5:28-32). When I was growing up, this subject was taboo. It certainly was never mentioned from the pulpit, but wake up church! If we do not address it from God's perspective, our kids are going to get caught in the trap! The wrong message about sex comes at children of all ages and from many angles. Prime-time TV tries to show our kids that everybody does it with whomever they want, at anytime. They are also witnessing gay and lesbian couples "getting married" and parading their perversion in public. Unfortunately, the world has a warped, perverted view of sex that if done according to its standards (or should I say lack of standards?) will lead to destruction. Paul shows the progression:

Romans 1:24-28 (NIV)

"Therefore God gave them over in the sinful desires of their hearts to sexual impurity for the degrading of their bodies with one another. [25] They exchanged the truth of God for a lie, and worshiped and served created things rather than the Creator—who is forever praised. Amen.

[26] Because of this, God gave them over to shameful lusts. Even their women exchanged natural relations for unnatural ones. [27] In the same way the men also abandoned natural relations with women and were inflamed with lust for one another. Men committed indecent acts with other men, and received in themselves the due penalty for their perversion.

[28] Furthermore, since they did not think it worthwhile to retain the knowledge of God, he gave them over to a depraved mind, to do what ought not to be done."

This may be the worst violation of the use of our senses. In the Old Testament, the misuse of sex led to the destruction of the people in Noah's day and in Sodom and Gomorrah. Our culture is going down the same path at an alarming rate.

No, the answer is not to pass out condoms to our kids because they are "going to do it anyway." That is not true! When we say that, we are showing that we do not believe in our kids. There is still a remnant of teens who want to be sold out to God! God lays out guidelines, not to make us uncomfortable, but to protect us. If we follow His guidelines, we will never have a sexually transmitted disease! Not only that, when we wait for the mate God has chosen for us (one man together with one woman)—and wait until marriage for sex after we find God's choice—we will experience the best sex! Guilt-free sex!

Yes, God is a redeeming God, and He's a God of second chances. No matter what you have done sexually, He can make you pure again. But we need to tell our teens God's plan for sex so they can remain pure and not have to go through all of that. God is a rewarder of those who diligently seek Him (Hebrews 11:16). Our message to the youth of our day should be, "Seek Him while you are young, then your desire to please Him will outweigh your desire to be sexually active, and He will reward you with the awesome gift of sex between one man and one woman within the confines of marriage."

The message to married women—especially faithful Christian women—should be, "Yes, God wants you to experience sex in the marriage bed to the fullest!" Many God-fearing women have a problem separating their spirituality from their sexuality. Because of that, some women limit what they feel in the marriage bed and allow their mind to "turn it off." God would not have made us with the ability to experience sexual pleasure if He did not intend for us to enjoy it.

The message to married men should be, "Love your wife as God loves the church; then your wife will respond sexually." What men need to remember is that women usually need tender, loving care. Sometimes that tender, loving care comes in the form of non-sexual physical affection. Other times, as crazy as this sounds to a man, tender, loving care comes in the form of taking out the trash, picking up his underwear, or tending the children without her help!

This beautiful act of two people merging in spirit, soul and body is allowed in the purity of the marriage bed—not allowing anyone else to enter, whether physically in the flesh or mentally in the mind. That is adultery, and it will destroy what God has intended. One time when we were stopped at a red light, my husband, Bill, was kissing me. My daughter Amber said, "Daddy, stop kissing on Mommy!" My other daughter, Amy, said, "Let them do it, Amber. They're committing marriage!"

Though marriage is a gift from God, we need to remember that our "completeness" comes from Christ alone! It is not true that we arc incomplete unless we are married. Singles need to put their trust in God. The message to singles should be, "Only God knows what is right for your life, whether He wants you to be sold out to Him as a single, or whether He has someone special picked out just for you. Either way, you can experience intimacy with Christ that far exceeds intimacy you could ever have with a person." Unmarried individuals do not need to allow their desire for a spouse to be a distraction from being able to be used of God in the season of their singleness. He may have glorious "God appointments" planned for them that they can only accomplish because they *are* single. As they seek God, He will start unfolding their life so beautifully—like He does the petals of a rose!

Misuse of sex is definitely a hindrance to true worship. I do not think people worship God while they are in the midst of a sexual act outside of marriage. On the other hand, I know you can worship God at the same time as coming together in the marriage bed with your spouse. Why wouldn't you be able to? As was mentioned earlier, God uses the union of man and wife as an illustration of Christ and His bride, the Church:

> "In the same way, husbands ought to love their wives as they love their own bodies. For a man is actually loving himself when he loves his wife. [29] No one hates his own body but lovingly cares for it, just as Christ cares for his body, which is the church. [30] And we are his body. [31] As the Scriptures say, 'A man leaves his father and mother and is joined to his wife, and the two are united into one.' [32] This is a great mystery, but it is an illustration of the way Christ and the church are one." Ephesians 5:28-32 (NLT)

Though the perversion of sex is the most obvious misuse of the sense of touch that hinders our worship of God, another misuse is when we use our hands to do things that are not pleasing to God. There are people, especially in tribal communities, who use their hands to make images to worship. "And there you will serve gods, the work of men's hands, wood and stone, which neither see nor hear nor eat nor smell" (Deuteronomy 4:28).

Most of us can say that we have never carved a god out of wood and worshiped it. However, how many of us are addicted to the work of our hands at our job? Sometimes we begin to take pride in the works of our hands and forget that God is our source, and that without Him we can do nothing. When we forget that, we are not worshiping Him.

> "...then you say in your heart, 'My power and the might of my hand have gained me this wealth.' [18] And you shall remember the Lord your God, for it is He who gives you power to get wealth, that He may establish His

covenant which He swore to your fathers, as it is this day."
Deuteronomy 8:17-18

One day all the things that are hidden will be brought to light.
God knows the motives of our heart. It is best to let Him show us
those hidden heart motives that are not pleasing to Him and let Him
deal with them. Then we will one day be able to stand before His
throne with clean hands and a pure heart!

Going Deeper

The truth about sexual immorality

1 Thessalonians 4:3-8 (NIV)

"It is God's will that you should be sanctified: that you should avoid
sexual immorality; [4] that each of you should learn to control his
own body in a way that is holy and honorable, [5] not in passionate
lust like the heathen, who do not know God; [6] and that in this
matter no one should wrong his brother or take advantage of him.
The Lord will punish men for all such sins, as we have already told
you and warned you. [7] For God did not call us to be impure, but
to live a holy life. [8] Therefore, he who rejects this instruction does
not reject man but God, who gives you his Holy Spirit."

Verse 3: What way does it list for you to be sanctified or set apart?

Verse 4: What does this verse say we should do?

Verse 5: Who takes part in sexual immorality?

Verse 6: What will God do to those who take advantage of someone
through the act of sexual immorality?

Verse 7: "God did not call us to _____, but to
_____."

Verse 8: Whom do people reject when they fall into the trap of sexual immorality?

Do you remember when Joseph was tempted by Potiphar's wife? (See Genesis 39.) In Genesis 39:9, whom did Joseph say he would be sinning against if he committed the sexual sin with her?

According to Proverbs 6:32, what does a person lack who commits adultery?

What does he destroy?

When we know God and realize that our bodies are the temples of the Holy Spirit, we will not want to do anything in our bodies that displeases Him. Read 1 Corinthians 6:19-20. (It is worth being reminded that the Greek word for "temple," *naos,* is the same word used for the Holy of Holies, the part of the temple that only the high priests could enter and where the Ark of the Covenant was kept.)

You may ask, "But what if I've already been guilty of sexual immorality. What now?" Good news! God is a God of second chances! If you want to be free from the guilt of sexual immorality, you need to do these things:

1. Confess your sin and ask God to break any ties to anyone with whom you have had a sexual relationship. According to 1 Corinthians 6:15-18, you become "one" with whomever you have sexual intercourse. Both people in the act actually are giving part of themselves to each other. Pray a prayer like this one taken from the book *Intimate Issues,* by Linda Dillow and Lorraine Pintus:

    "Dear Heavenly Father,

    I know that it was sinful and offensive to You when I committed sexual immorality by (offense) with (name of person). I understand that by this sexual act I joined my spirit together with _____'s spirit. I ask that You forgive me for (offense) and that you break this spiritual union with _____. Grant me spiritual freedom from _____ and return my spirit to me. I ask that the blood of Jesus would cleanse my spirit as it returns to me. I pray that the door of sensual thought and action toward _____ will be closed forever. Dear God, make me spiritually whole again. This I pray by faith and through the power of Jesus. Amen."[1]

2. Forgive yourself. If you do not forgive yourself even though God has, you are placing yourself above God. Read, underline and memorize 1 John 1:9.

3. The enemy would love to keep the condemning thoughts coming.

What does 2 Corinthians 10:4-5 say we can do with the weapons God gives us?

Sometimes in the midst of tormenting thoughts, we need to stop, pray, declare that the strongholds of the thoughts are cast down and ask God to remind us of a truth from His Word to replace those thoughts. You may need to do that right now in your journal. Write down any lie or tormenting thought you are having (whether it is dealing with sex or not), and next to it, write a truth from God's Word that will answer that lie.

The Act of Marriage, a Beautiful Gift!
Only God could create such an awesome gift as the gift of intimacy in marriage where a man and a woman can come together and become one in spirit, soul and body. He also included a whole book in the Bible devoted to love, romance and marital intimacy. You can check it out for yourself in Song of Solomon, especially chapter 4.

In Hebrews 13:4, what does it say about the marriage bed?

In 1 Corinthians 7:3-5, Paul instructs us that sex is actually our duty to each other as man and wife. According to this passage, when is it OK to have an extended period of time in which we refrain from sexual intercourse with our spouse?

Why do we need to come back together after that period of time?

Before you can have intimacy, you have to have trust. What we need to remember is that God wants us to trust Him, not man. When you get to know God, you will trust Him because He is faithful! When you trust Him, you will be able to give your all to your spouse, because God will not let you down. Read the following scriptures and write down what they are saying to you about trusting God:
Psalm 9:10 -

Psalm 125:1 -

Jeremiah 17:7,8 -

Works of Hands
"Woe to the wicked! Disaster is upon them! They will be paid back for what their hands have done." Isaiah 3:11 (NIV)

What does this verse say that the wicked will be paid back for?

What does Psalm 9:16 say about the wicked?

Not only does God punish those who do evil acts with their hands, but He also rewards those who do not. Read Psalm 18:24.

Read Psalm 24:3-4. Who will be able to stand in God's holy place?

Prayer

Lord, I choose this day to trust in You, because You are faithful! It is Your goodness that leads me to repentance, and for that I am grateful. Forgive me for the ways I have sinned against you in the area of touch. I know this has hindered my worship. Please restore my sexuality in the way You intend it to be. I pray this day for clean hands and a pure heart so that I may be able to bask in Your presence. I know as I trust in You, You will take care of every aspect of my life. I love You!

The Sense of Touch

Day 3

Not Allowing Anyone to Touch Us
Is a Big Mistake!

Some people want to be "untouchable"—and that is the biggest hindrance they have to loving God and others. Why does this happen? One reason is because they have been hurt, and they do not want to be hurt again. They do not want anyone to be able to touch them. They need a healing touch from the Master before they can get close to anyone.

Another reason people do not want to get close to others is that they are concerned about their reputation. Why are we so concerned about what people think of us? We need to be more concerned about how we represent Christ than we are about our reputations. I like what Paul wrote in Galatians 1:10 (NIV): "Am I now trying to win the approval of men, or of God? Or am I trying to please man? If I were still trying to please men, I would not be a servant of Christ."

People who are hurt and continue to worry about their reputation instead of their representation of Christ will react one of two ways. They will either have a victim mentality or they will become hardened and angry. Either way, they are not allowing anyone, including God, to touch them. The person with a victim mentality will wallow in self-pity and pull away from others, while the person who has developed a hardness of heart gives out a message that no one will control him again.

In either case, the person who does not want anyone to "touch" him is focused on himself. That is pride. As we learned in Day 5 of "Taste," the letter "I" is the center of pride, and pride is the center of every sin. Every sin you can think of is self-centered. What we need to remember is that it is not about us!

2 Corinthians 4:7-11

"But we have this treasure in earthen vessels, *that the excellence of the power may be of God and not of us.* [8] We are hard pressed on every side, yet not crushed; we are perplexed, but not in despair; [9] persecuted, but not forsaken; struck down, but not destroyed — [10] always carrying about in the body the dying of the Lord Jesus, that the life of Jesus also may be manifested in our body. [11] For we who live are always delivered to death for Jesus' sake, that the life of Jesus also may be manifested in our mortal flesh." (Emphasis added)

When we remember this truth — that it is not about us — we will not wallow in misery, but instead we will allow God to take care of the situation as only He can.

One of the enemy's first tactics to get us down is to isolate us. When you are going through trials, you may be tempted to stay home and not go to church. You can be a Christian and not go to church, but it is hard! If you follow through with the temptation to stay away from church, you are forgetting that as believers in Christ, we encourage one another in the faith. Solomon lets us know in Ecclesiastes 4:9-12 that two are better than one, because if one falls, the other one will help him up. In verse 10, he says, "...but woe to him who is alone when he falls, for he has no one to help him up." When you stop going to church, it is like taking a coal from the fire and seeing the flame die. Hebrews 10:25 says, "Let us not give up meeting together, as some are in the habit of doing, but let us encourage one another — and all the more as you see the Day approaching."

Usually the next step after not attending church is to isolate yourself from God as well. That is when we lose our peace, because He is our peace! "I will both lie down in peace, and sleep; for You alone, O Lord, make me dwell in safety" (Psalm 4:8).

The truth is that Jesus was isolated so that we do not have to be. Some people who have isolated themselves from others, and even from God, are just broken and need a healing touch from God. They may have been betrayed by a friend. They may have just experienced the loss of a loved one through death. We need to look for these people. Is there someone you know at your church whom you have not seen for a while? They may need an encouraging phone call or a visit to let them know that someone cares. Or maybe you are that broken person. Know that Jesus went through major rejection and sorrow, and He understands what you are going through. Though He is the healer, He oftentimes uses other people to pour His love and blessings on you. Let Him. One day you will have that same opportunity to reach out to someone else who is hurting.

"Each of us has something broken in our lives; a broken promise, a broken dream, a broken marriage, a broken heart...and we must decide how we're going to deal with our brokenness. We can wallow in self-pity or regret, accomplishing nothing and having no fun or joy in our circumstances; or we can determine with our will to take a few risks, get out of our comfort zone, and see what God will do to bring unexpected delight in our time of need." Luci Swindoll[1]

Going Deeper

Reputation or Representation

It is our human nature to be concerned about our reputation, but we need to get past that. We cannot be concerned about our reputation and represent Christ at the same time because He made Himself of no reputation. Yes, we might need to be concerned whether or not the character of Christ is in us. However, even if we worry about this too much, we start becoming self-focused instead of God-focused. We just need to spend time with God. As we do, He will develop character in us, and He will bring those people He wants into our life and let others go.

After reading Philippians 2:5-8, write out a prayer that God will help you in this area.

Note: When you do this, you will not get puffed up when someone brags about you, and you will not get depressed when someone slanders you. In either case, you bow before your Heavenly Father and commit it to Him. What a release!

We Need Each Other!
Read Romans 12:3-18 and answer these questions:

Verse 3 - What is the first step in getting along with others in the church?

Verses 4 & 5 - "...we have _____ members in _____ _____ body..."

Verses 6-8 - These verses list "motivational gifts." Everyone has at least one of these gifts, thus all the needs are met within the church! When you read this list, which gift is stirred in you more than the others?

Verse 9 - What does this verse say about love?

Verse 10 - This verse tells us how to love. What does it say?

Verses 11-18 – This passage lists many ways in which God wants His people to relate to each other. As you allow the Holy Spirit to minister to you through these verses, document what He is speaking to your heart.

(For further study on the church being many members, but one body, you may also see 1 Corinthians 12:12-27.)

Remember what was mentioned in Day 1 of Touch, how Peter called members of the body of Christ "living stones" in 1 Peter 2:5. Think about stonework on a building. The stones are fit together perfectly—not as bricks all uniform and the same—but as unique stones with different sizes and shapes that fit together like a puzzle! This week, allow God to remind you of specific people in your church for whom you need to thank Him and ask Him to bless them. Try to think of people who might not be so obvious.

He was isolated so that we don't have to be!
Read Isaiah 53:3-6 below and answer the following questions:

Isaiah 53:3-6

He is despised and rejected by men,
A Man of sorrows and acquainted with grief.
And we hid, as it were, our faces from Him;
He was despised, and we did not esteem Him.
[4] Surely He has borne our griefs
And carried our sorrows;
Yet we esteemed Him stricken,
Smitten by God, and afflicted.
[5] But He was wounded for our transgressions,
He was bruised for our iniquities;
The chastisement for our peace was upon Him,
And by His stripes we are healed.
[6] All we like sheep have gone astray;
We have turned, every one, to his own way;
And the Lord has laid on Him the iniquity of us all.

Verse 3 - What did Jesus experience from men?

He received rejection from us as well. Notice how the author used the word "we" in the second part of the verse. In the New Living

Translation, it says, "We turned our backs on him and looked the other way when he went by. He was despised, and we did not care."

Verse 4 - Jesus bore our _____ and carried our _____ on the cross. Yet there have been times that instead of thanking Him, we esteemed Him stricken. Next time you see a crucifix, instead of just thinking about His pain on the cross, thank Him. He did it for you!

Verse 5 – Underline the verse above. You may want to memorize it.

Verse 6 - How many have turned away from God?
How many people's sins did Jesus take on Himself when He died on the cross?

Prayer

Oh, precious Lord Jesus, thank You so much for what You did for me on Calvary. Please forgive me for the times I have turned away from You and others in your body. I turn to You now! You suffered rejection, sorrow and grief because of Your unconditional love for me! You were crushed, and now You are close to those whose hearts are crushed. You were wounded for my iniquities, and now my sins can be forgiven. You were chastised, and now I can have peace. You were whipped with a "cat of nine tails," and now I can be healed! The words "thank you" are not enough to express my gratitude to You. May my life be such that I can point other people, who are turning their faces away from you, toward You! In Your Name I pray, Amen!

The Sense of Touch

Day 4

Loving People, Loving God

W e eat the fruit of our lips, which are our words (Proverbs 18:20-21). Consequently, taste also involves what we say, which naturally affect how we "touch" someone relationally. As an example, a friend of mine once came to me and said, "The Lord has been convicting me of saying, 'I *nailed* them!' Jesus was nailed to the cross. You know that hurts! I started thinking about it and realized that when I said that, I meant that I had hurt someone with my words."

The Bible makes it clear that when we show love to people, we show love to God (Matthew 25:40). We are also warned that we cannot say we love God whom we do not see if we hate our brother whom we do see (1 John 4:20). Each person is very special to God. If we love God, we will treasure what He treasures—that is, people!

Each one of us is the "apple of His eye" (Psalm 17:8, Zechariah 2:8). What is the "apple of the eye?" It is the very center opening called the pupil. Figuratively speaking, it is something, or more commonly someone, who is cherished above others.[1] Think about it. Have you ever been poked in the eye? It hurts! When we talk negatively about someone or treat him harshly, it is as if we are sticking our finger in God's eye!

That is why we need to start being more sensitive to the leading of the Holy Spirit before we speak. This week, make an effort to check your words before you speak. Are they words that will edify and build up or words that will tear down? There are two agendas: Satan's agenda to steal, kill and destroy, and God's agenda to give life and give it more abundantly. With which agenda are your words lining up?

Before we speak, we need to ask ourselves the following questions:

1.) **Are we saying the right thing?** Many times people speak without knowing the whole story. If we offer our opinion before we have all the information, we could hurt someone.

2.) **Are we saying it to the right person?** Sometimes we may need to address a situation, but we talk to someone who does not need to know. Bringing in a third party might cause additional offense.

3.) **Are we saying it at the right time?** There is an old saying that "Timing is everything!" Communication is a two-way street. If the other person is not ready to receive our words, we could do more harm than good.

4.) **Are we saying it in the right way?** Nonverbal communication is as important as verbal. Our words might say one thing; our tone of voice and body language might be saying another.

Actions speak louder than words. Not only do we need to speak words that will build up and edify, but we also need to show our love to others by our actions. I highly respect the Salvation Army. They say that you must first show someone love through acts of service before they will listen to the Gospel message. How often are we as Christians just sitting in our comfort zone, fellowshipping with other believers at church while there is a lost and dying world outside the walls of the church?

Compassion does something. Think of the biblical story of the Good Samaritan. (See Luke 10: 30-37.) A priest and a Levite saw a wounded man who had been attacked by robbers and they passed by without helping him. Both of them represent "religious" people. Levites assisted the priests in the temple. Even though Jews and Samaritans did not normally get along, the Samaritan saw the wounded man and showed compassion by stopping to treat his wounds, taking him to get help and paying all the bills. He did not show any concerns or expectations about being repaid.

Whether it is in the mission field in a foreign land or right in our own community, there are opportunities for each of us become involved in reaching hurting people with God's love. We don't want to just "do" out of feelings of guilt or because it is expected of us. But as we get closer to the Lord, He will stir our hearts and let us know the assignments He has for us. He just might start stirring a passion in your heart for those in prisons, nursing homes, homeless shelters, or in backyard Bible clubs for kids! He might put a ministry on your heart that He wants you to support with your prayers and finances. He will then be using you to play a part in fulfilling the Great Commission and touching others with the love of Christ!

> " 'And Jesus came and spoke to them, saying, "All
> authority has been given to Me in heaven and on earth.
> [19] Go therefore and make disciples of all the nations,
> baptizing them in the name of the Father and of the Son and
> of the Holy Spirit, [20] teaching them to observe all things
> that I have commanded you; and lo, I am with you always,
> even to the end of the age.' Amen."
> Matthew 28:18-20

Going Deeper

We Are the Apple of His Eye!
Being the apple of His eye means you are most precious to Him. He has His eye on you! He knows where you are and what you are going through.

Read Psalm 17:8 and make it your prayer today.

What does God ask us to keep as the apple of our eye in Proverbs 7:2?

What do you think is our reward when we do that?

Read Zechariah 2:8 below. It talks of the Jews, God's chosen people:

"For thus says the Lord of hosts: He sent Me after glory, to the nations which plunder you; for he who touches you touches the apple of His eye." Zechariah 2:8

We can also apply this verse to us, because according to Romans 2:29, we are also "Jews" if we have our hearts "circumcised": "but he is a Jew who is one inwardly; and circumcision is that of the heart, in the Spirit, not in the letter; whose praise is not from men but from God" (Romans 2:29).

Look back at the last part of Zechariah 2:8, and fill in the blanks: ... for he who _____ you touches _____.

We need to remember this when we are tempted to talk negatively about someone. If we remember that we are "sticking our finger in God's eye," we will be less likely to hurt another individual. In a literal sense, we need to pray that our country will stand behind the Jewish homeland of Israel. One day God's judgment will come against all those who are against Israel (Psalm 122:6).

Be Careful What You Say!

Note: We have already dealt with this subject on Day 3 of "Taste," but it is most definitely an important topic that is worth continued study. The words that come from the mouth will either help to promote our relationship with God or be a hindrance to having intimacy with Him (Matthew 12:37).

Read James 3:4-10 and answer these questions:
Verse 4 – What does the *small* rudder on a ship do?

Verse 5 – To what is the tongue, being "a *little* member and boasts great things," likened?

Verse 6 – One person's words can defile the whole body! This verse says that the fire of the tongue is set on fire by _____.

Verses 7 & 8 – Man can tame every kind of wild animal, but cannot tame the tongue. That is why we must rely on God to help us! What does this say that the tongue is full of?

Verse 9 – What does this verse say we do with our tongues toward God?

What does the verse say we do with our tongues toward other people who are created in God's image?

Verse 10 – What does this verse say is not right?

Compassion Touches People!
James 2:16 reminds us to back up our words with action. What comes to your mind after you read that verse?

Sometimes God wants us to actually do something ourselves, but sometimes all we can do is bring the person to Christ. Read Mark 2:1-12. Four men were moved with compassion for one man who was a paralytic. What did they do?

When Jesus saw their faith, what did He do?

When the scribes accused Him of blasphemy, because only God can forgive sins, what did Jesus do that proved His deity?

Just think, the faith of the four friends, who had compassion and wanted to take the paralytic to the only One who could help him, led to the man's salvation and healing! Not only that, but they all glorified God!

Prayer

Lord, in everything I say and do, may my life bring glory to You! I want to be able to bring a healing touch to hurting people with my words and actions. Please forgive me of every idle word and for the times I have not served someone with acts of service when You have prompted me. Help me to hear and obey Your Spirit as You lead me in what to say and do.

The Sense of Touch

Day 5

Worship from Our Whole Being

Touch brings about feeling. When my daughter was in preschool, she made a "touching" book. Each page had something to touch and a word that described what it felt like when you touched it. For instance, a piece of cotton was glued to one page with the word "soft" written under it; sandpaper was glued to another page with the word "rough" under it.

Touch has to happen before feeling comes. Someone might see a plush stuffed animal and know by experience that it feels soft and is very comfortable to cuddle, but he will not feel the softness until he actually handles it. The soft, comfortable feeling that comes from holding that plush stuffed animal is *not* the act of touching, but the feeling comes as soon as one actually picks it up and touches it. In the same way, the feeling one gets when worshiping God is not the worship, but it comes after reaching out and "touching" Him in worship.

We have already learned from Day 1 of "Touch" that this sense affects the whole body. No wonder it represents worship in the spiritual realm. Worship is more than just a twenty- to thirty-minute song service on Sunday morning. Worship is a lifestyle of honoring God with our whole being—spirit, soul and body. Sometimes we need to choose to worship even when we do not "feel" like it. When we do, the stresses of everyday life seem to stop controlling us. It is as though we crawl up into the Father's lap and let His embrace calm our fears, just as a mother's arms calm a crying baby. Then we *will* feel like worshiping.

True worship comes from the spirit. Our spirit is that part of us that communes with God—our inner core. Jesus said to the woman at the well in John 4:23-24, "But the hour is coming, and now is, when the true worshipers will worship the Father in spirit and truth; for the Father is seeking such to worship Him. God is Spirit, and those who worship Him must worship in spirit and truth." When that happens, our mindset and the emotions of our soul will be positively affected. Sometimes, we just cannot help but show it in our physical body as well, as we lift our hands to the Lord in adoration or even dance before Him.

However, we need to be cautious that we not try to "work up" those feelings of worship. I know that many times in a contemporary worship service, people may be moved by the music and even stirred emotionally but never reach the heart of God in true worship. We must not substitute the style of music we enjoy for true intimacy with God. Music is powerful. It can stir emotions and even bring goose bumps or move us to tears! Yes, God made music and oftentimes uses it to bring us to the throne room, but we should not put the emphasis on the tool God uses to bring us to Him. Our worship should not depend on a worship team! Our emphasis should be on Him alone. Remember, God is Spirit, and those who worship Him must worship Him in spirit and in truth. Only God can judge if someone is truly worshiping. 1 Samuel 16:7(b) reminds us that "...man looks at the outward appearance, but the Lord looks at the heart."

To those who are critical of Christians who show outward expressions in worship, I will remind you of the comfortable, plush stuffed animal. You will not experience what it is like to feel that soft, comfortable feeling until you actually pick it up and embrace it. It's OK! God made us with emotions. In His presence is fullness of joy and at His right hand are pleasures forevermore! (See Psalm 16:11.) I challenge you to be as the psalmist in Psalm 63:4: "Thus I will bless You while I live; I will lift up my hands in Your name."

What we all need to remember in the body of Christ is that worship is not just what happens in a church service. The Bible tells us to "love the Lord your God with all your heart, with all your soul, with all your mind, and with all your strength" (Deuteronomy 6:5 and Mark 12:30). I would call that a lifestyle! Worship comes in many different forms. You can set time aside to be alone with God and lie prostrate or kneel before Him, but you can also worship while you are on the go! When I was a child, my mother had a tremendously positive influence on me when she worshiped God in song and prayer while she did the dishes and the laundry. When you worship Him from the very core of your being, you will find opportunities to worship at times that you would not have even thought of before—like in a traffic jam or a doctor's waiting room. Sometimes you will have times of praising Him with your voice, while at other times just sitting quietly and meditating on His Word will bring honor to Him in your spirit.

At the beginning of this chapter I talked about how touching brings about feeling, as when you pick up a plush, stuffed animal and feel how soft it is. That is true if our nerve endings are working properly. However, some people have been damaged in their nervous system and cannot feel because they are paralyzed. In the same way, some people are paralyzed emotionally or spiritually. Some have been abused to such a degree that their emotional nerves have been damaged, and thus they have a hard time being able to feel true love and affection. In turn, they also do not know how to give true love and affection. We can also be deadened spiritually by sin so that we do not enter into worship, and thus we cannot receive God's true love and affection. If you have been hurt in your emotions, or if sin is keeping you from entering into true intimacy with God, turn to Him and ask Him to help you surrender to Him. Jesus came to heal the brokenhearted and restore us to Him. He said in Luke 18:4, "The Spirit of the Lord is upon Me, because He has anointed Me to preach the gospel to the poor; he has sent Me to heal the brokenhearted, to proclaim liberty to the captives and recovery of sight to the blind, to set at liberty those who are oppressed." When you allow Him to do that in your life, you will then be free to worship Him!

As you worship God, you will start becoming like Him. Think about how Jesus lived on this earth with such great wisdom. As you spend more time with God, He will give you His wisdom to also know how to live practically in this world.

"But seek (aim at and strive after) first of all His kingdom and His righteousness (His way of doing and being right), and then all these things taken together will be given you besides." Matthew 6:33 (AMP)

For many of you participating in this study, you are about to walk into a new level of getting to know God like never before! Go ahead and surrender—you will be so glad you did!

Going Deeper

True Worship
In your own words, what do you think worship is?

Look up and write the definition for "worship" from the dictionary.

Read John 4:21-26 and answer the following questions:

In verse 22, what did Jesus say about the worship of the Samaritans?

What did He say about the worship of the Jews?

Write out verse 23.

Note that God is seeking true worshipers!

In verse 24, Jesus reemphasized that "true worshipers will worship the Father in _____ and _____."

In his book, *With Christ in the School of Prayer*, Andrew Murray wrote:

To the woman of Samaria our Lord spoke of a threefold worship:

1. The ignorant worship of the Samaritans: "You Samaritans worship what you do not know"
2. The intelligent worship of the Jew, having the true knowledge of God: "We worship what we do know, for salvation is from the Jews"
3. The new, spiritual worship that He himself has come to introduce: "Yet a time is coming and has now come when the true worshipers will worship the Father in spirit and truth"[1]

1. The "ignorant worship of the Samaritans" reminds me of the worship of people who are not Christians. They do not know Jesus, who is the way, the truth and the life. They may even worship in sincerity, but sincere worship does not necessarily mean true worship.
2. The "intelligent worship of the Jew, having true knowledge of God" reminds me of Christians who "know" all the scriptures, but may not have an intimate relationship with God.
3. "The new, spiritual worship" originates from the Godhead. "True worshipers" will worship the <u>Father</u> in <u>spirit</u> (The Holy Spirit dwells in your spirit) and <u>truth</u> (Jesus is the truth). True worship is only in and through Jesus. The Father sent the Son, and the Spirit guides us to Jesus. Without Jesus, there is no true worship.

God is the only One worthy of our worship!

Psalm 135:15-18 tells us that you become like whatever you worship. That is why teenagers start dressing and acting like the rock stars they idolize. In this passage, what are the characteristics of the idols that the people who worship have?

    1.

    2.

3.

4.

In other words, there is no life in them!

What are the first two of the Ten Commandments? (See Exodus 20:3-4.)

An idol, or graven image, can be anything or anyone that we place above God. Can you think of some idols in your life that sometimes get in the way of your worship of God? If so, write out a prayer in your journal to confess them and ask God to help you get rid of those idols. In some cases, He may be asking you to physically throw something away. If He is, and you do it, tremendous peace will flood your soul, and you will feel that a tremendous weight has been lifted!

Peter did not receive worship. What did Peter say to Cornelius when Cornelius fell down at Peter's feet to worship him in Acts 10:25-26?

In Revelation 22:8-9, why do you think John fell down to worship the angel?

What did the angel tell him?

Preparation of the one who worships

Sin in our life can hinder our worship. What did the Israelites do in Nehemiah 9:2-3 before they read the scriptures and before they worshiped?

Read Psalm 100:4 and think about how we should enter His gates to praise and worship Him and what attitude we should have.

Just as we learned in Day 4 of "Touch" that we should not just talk about helping someone, but we should put actions to our words, so it is with worshiping God as well.

"The Lord says:
'These people come near to me with their mouth
and honor me with their lips,
but their hearts are far from me.
Their worship of me
is made up only of rules taught by men.' "
Isaiah 29:13

Prayer

Today's ending prayer needs to come from you! Write out a prayer. If time permits, you may want to go into a time of worship after that. Do whatever He stirs you to do. He may want you to play soft worship music and get alone with Him or go for a walk with Him as you pray and worship. May God bless your time with Him!

The Sense of Sight

"So Jesus had compassion and touched their eyes.
And immediately their eyes received sight, and they
followed Him." Matthew 20:34

Day 1

Sight: Let There Be Light

The eye is absolutely one of the most intriguing organs of the body—so much so that sight is considered the most complex of our five senses. After studying the eye, it is hard to imagine how anyone can believe there is not a Creator who is responsible for such an intelligent, complex design! According to an article entitled "The Evolution of Life, Probability Considerations and Common Sense," by Dr. John Ankerberg and Dr. John Weldon, "The optic nerve has about one million fibers, and these may be connected to the brain in one million factorial ways. The odds they could have been connected correctly by chance cannot even be written out long hand."[1] It is not by chance that we have two eyes instead of one, either. God created us with two eyes so that we would be able to see three dimensionally. Let's look more closely at how the eye works.

When an object is seen, light rays bounce off of the object and enter the eye through the cornea. The cornea, the part on the front of the eye that protrudes slightly, is a transparent protective layer on the eye's surface. The chamber made by the protrusion of the cornea is filled with transparent fluid that includes oxygen, protein and glucose to keep the eye healthy.

After the light rays pass through the cornea, they go through the opening in the center of the eye called the pupil. The iris is the ring around the pupil that has color. The muscles of the iris contract and expand to adjust the size of the pupil to the amount of light that is needed. When it is dark, the pupil is larger to let in more light; when the light is bright, the pupil is smaller to let in less light.

The light then passes through the lens and into the back of the eye onto the retina. The lens is held in place by a bunch of fibers attached to the ciliary muscle, which changes the shape of the lens in order to focus.

Before the light rays reach the retina, they pass through an area called the vitreous humor that contains a jelly-like substance. This area makes up two-thirds of the eye and gives the eyeball its shape.

The retina is only about as big as a thumbnail but contains about 150 million light-sensitive cells called rods and cones. Rods identify shapes and black and white, while cones identify color. The retina changes the light rays into nerve signals and sends them to the brain by way of the optic nerve. When the image is sent to the brain, it is upside down. The brain then turns it right side up and interprets what is seen. This is done in the part of the brain called the visual cortex.

The eyes are such an important part of the body that God has made sure that they are protected. The eyelids help to protect our eyes from injuries. Eyelashes help keep out small dirt and dust particles. The eyebrows help keep our sweat from flowing into the eyes.

God even made our eyes with their own cleansing process. When a foreign object does enter the eye, sterile drops of clean water, better known as tears, wash the object out of the eye. Tears also keep the eye moist. Every time we blink, a tiny bit of tear fluid flows. Most people blink once every two to 10 seconds, with a blink lasting for about three-tenths of a second. That means we have our eyes closed at least a half an hour a day just from blinking!

We do not shed tears just to clean out foreign objects; we also cry when our emotions are triggered. The same emotions that cause our skin to react with sweat or goose bumps also cause our eyes to start crying. There are tears of sadness, fear, grief, sorrow and joy. The enemy of our souls would love for us to take on his perspective of tears—that is to cry because there is no hope. However, God made us with the ability to release stress through tears. He sees every tear and cares about we care about (1 Peter 5:7). According to Revelation 7:17, one day He will wipe away every tear from our eyes!

As we study the sense of sight, we find that it is such an incredible gift from God that helps us function in life. Spiritually speaking, it is imperative for us to have sight to know how to live in this world of darkness. Just as we stumble and fall in the darkness, we will stumble in life if we do not have God's Word to be the lamp to our feet and the light to our path (Psalm 119:105). In John 8:12, Jesus tells us, "I am the light of the world. He who follows Me shall not walk in darkness, but have the light of life." Praise God that He actually guides us to live a life of peace, joy and contentment no matter what comes our way! With His light we get to see the storms coming and are guided through them!

Going Deeper

The Beauty of Creation

> "Then God saw everything that He had made, and indeed it was very good. So the evening and the morning were the sixth day." Genesis 1:31

Too often we get so caught up in our busy routines that we forget to look at the beauty of God's creation all around us. When we do take the time, it should remind us of how great God is! Read the following passages from Psalms about God's creation and journal your response:

Psalm 19:1	Psalm 24:1-2	Psalm 95:3-5
Psalm 104:1-26	Psalm 136:4-9	Psalm 139:7-16

Read Romans 1:18-20. In your own words, tell how creation plays a part in pointing our attention to God.

From Tears to Triumph

As we have seen in Psalms, David was awed and humbled by seeing the beauty of God's creation and he gave God the praise and honor due unto Him. However, David was not always upbeat. There were many times he wrote about his sorrows. The following scriptures are examples:

Psalm 6:6   Psalm 42:3   Psalm 56:8

It is all right to cry! God has wonderfully created us with the ability to physically release our emotional turmoil through tears. Our society often sends the message that we are not supposed to cry—especially to men. However, sometimes tears can be a great release and can lead to victory.

Read Hebrews 5:7. To whom does this verse refer?

Do you think Jesus trusted the Father?

Just because we cry does not mean we do not trust God. In Day 5 of "Taste," we learned how we sometimes have to suffer if we want to know God intimately. God will let you know if your tears are because of a lack of trust, or if your tears are actually leading you closer to Him.

Read Psalm 84:5-7 and answer the following questions:

Verse 5 – If you want to be blessed, where does your strength need to be?

Where should your heart be set?

(In other words, remember that this world is not your home; you are just passing through!)

Verse 6 – You will pass through the valley of _____.
(Note: "Baca" means tears.)

What will it end up being?

Get in the Word, rely on God, and pray. Then your valley of tears will be a spring, and the Lord will rain down His Living Water upon you so much that there will be pools around you! Spring up, oh well, within my soul!

Verse 7 – You will go from _____ to _____.

These times when our tears lead to triumph are also when we are being transformed into God's image from glory to glory, as Paul says:

"But we all, with unveiled face, beholding as in a mirror the glory of the Lord, are being transformed into the same image from glory to glory, just as by the Spirit of the Lord." 2 Corinthians 3:18

Read Psalm 126:5-6 and answer these questions:
Verse 5 – If you sow in tears, what will you reap?

Verse 6 – What does it say one is doing "who continually goes forth weeping"?

After the tears, what will happen?

Good news! There is coming a day when crying will cease!

Read Revelation 21:1-4 and write out verse 4.

Changed in the Twinkling of an Eye
According to 1 Corinthians 15:51-52, when Jesus comes to take the church, how long will it take to be changed?
Just think, that is three-tenths of a second!

Read Revelation 1:7. How many will see Jesus when He comes in the clouds?

Until that day, we must share the light of Jesus to the lost and dying world.

Darkness and Light

So many people are walking around in darkness not even aware of what is going on in the spiritual realm—or that the spiritual realm even exists. This lack of light leads to immorality such that people start calling evil good and good evil. Isaiah 5:20 says, "Woe to those who call evil good, and good evil; who put darkness for light, and light for darkness; who put bitter for sweet, and sweet for bitter!" That speaks of the condition of the world today—a world of people in darkness desperate for light.

When Jesus came to the earth, the world was in much darkness and in need of light. There were 400 years of silence from God in between the time of the Old Testament and when Jesus was born. The world was in desperate need of light. It was time for prophesies of the coming Messiah to be fulfilled (Galatians 4:4). One of those prophesies is found in Isaiah 9:2: "The people who walked in darkness have seen a great light; those who dwelt in the land of the shadow of death, upon them a light has shined."

Read John 8:12. Jesus identified Himself as the light of the world. Write down Jesus' words in this verse.

The world we live in has much darkness today. Those of us who have Jesus in our hearts are also light to the world. Read the following verses about our lives being light and write down what these verses are saying to you:
Matthew 5:14-16 -

Romans 13:12-14 -

1 Peter 2:9 -

1 John 2:9-11 -

Isaiah 50:10 -

Prayer

Thank you, Lord, for the way you created my eyes and blessed me with sight! Please remind me to step back from my busy life-style and think about the beauty of the things I see. All the beauty of nature reflects Your glory, oh Lord! Thank You for the blessed hope of the church when You will come for us in the clouds. We will be changed in the twinkling of an eye, and we will all be together in Heaven, where You will wipe away every tear! Until then, I pray that I will be a light to the lost, so that they, too, can follow You and have the light of life.

The Sense of Sight

Day 2

Misuse Hinders Our Vision and Purpose

M y daughters love shopping in dollar stores. When they go in, I have to give them a time limit *and* a spending limit because they want to buy everything they see! It's like the list from the song in *The Sound of Music* entitled "My Favorite Things"—they love so many things they see, they usually have a very hard time deciding what to choose! I do not know if it is more of a lesson for them in self-control and decision-making, or a lesson for me in patience!

Some people are like that when they eat at a buffet. Jokes are made that they are on a "see-food diet"—they eat everything they see! Then they walk out with their hand on their belly saying, "Oh, I'm so full. I think my eyes were bigger than my stomach!"

As we learned on Day 1 of "Sight," our eyes are very complex and enable us to see great details and contrasts in color, texture and dimension. From the very moment we wake in the morning and open our sleepy eyes, our sense of sight is in operation. Understandably, there are also many distractions that come with seeing that can keep our minds focused on the natural instead of the spiritual. That is why most of the time we need to close our eyes while we pray, so we will not have so many distractions. (However, as you grow in the Lord, you will find that you can pray with your eyes open more often, because you learn not to let the things you see be a distraction.) In 2 Corinthians 4, Paul brings things into perspective for us. The last verse of the chapter urges us to look past what we see with our "natural eyes." 2 Corinthians 4:18: "So we fix our eyes not on what is seen, but on what is unseen. For what is seen is temporary, but what is unseen is eternal."

It is said that the eye is the "window to the soul." There are two sides to every window. We can look out, and others can look in. Looking out, we see things and immediately make judgments. We must come against our natural tendency to form opinions at first sight. Sometimes when I cook vegetables, one of my daughters will come into the kitchen and see what is on the stove. Immediately she will say, "Do I have to eat that?" Most of the time, she will make that judgment before she ever takes a taste. People do that when they see someone for the first time. Just by looking, they will make judgments about a person based solely on appearance. Like the saying goes, "Don't judge a book by its cover." That saying is actually scriptural! Its basis can be found in the Old Testament, 1 Samuel 16:7: "... the Lord does not see as man sees; for man looks at the outward appearance, but the Lord looks at the heart."

Another thing we need to remember about looking out of the window with our spiritual eyes is that we have a limited view. Even if we look out of a huge picture window, we can only see a portion of the total scene. And even if we walk out of the building to see more, we still will not see everything, because we all have blind spots. It is like when someone is driving a car: If he does not remember that he has a blind spot in his field of vision, he could have a wreck while changing lanes on a busy highway.

We need to keep this in mind in our relationships. We might think we know all the facts, but key information might be hidden in our personal blind spot. People bump into each other all the time, because they react out of their woundedness instead of responding in a way that is pleasing to the Lord. Each person interprets the other's reaction in the context of his own wounds and reacts accordingly. All the while, neither person sees what is in the other person's heart that would trigger a negative reaction. God is the only one who sees all and knows all. That is why we must ask God to show us His perspective and the perspective of others before we make any judgments.

The things that we do see can lead us down the wrong road if we are not careful. We have many visual mediums today: television, computers DVD players, camera phones, etc. It was only in the 1950s that color TV was introduced. Yet today we can sit in a comfortable chair just about anywhere in public or in private with a laptop and access sites on the Internet within seconds. With the increase in technology in the computer industry, the number of households with Internet connection is on the rise.

The porn industry, with its perversion, has also taken advantage of the World Wide Web and "spam" e-mail. Without proper blocks in place, our children can be visiting an innocent children's web site, or even checking e-mail, when a pornographic picture will pop up. It only takes once and an addiction can be started. This addiction can be harder to break than drug addiction, because the images are stored in the brain and can be recalled at any time. We need to wake up and see just how serious this problem is! Pornography is rampant all around us and is leading to an increase in violence and a desensitizing to this country's moral fiber. According to an article entitled "Pornography: Harmless Fun or Public Health Hazard?" by Daniel Weiss on the Focus on the Family website (www.family.org), this addiction has a direct impact on the breakdown of the family with an increase of divorces directly related to porn. Weiss' report also mentions the correlation between pornography and sexual violence crimes with the most common interest between serial killers being hardcore pornography. Sadly, this is not limited to adults, as 20-30% of the traffic to some porn websites are children, and worse than that, children as young as 8 years old are committing felony sexual crimes.[1] We need to be very careful and take every precaution we can to protect our children.

Unfortunately, this problem is also infiltrating the church. Ministers as well as others in leadership are falling into the enemy's trap of pornography. Focus on the Family has created a Web site (www.pureintimacy.org) especially for anyone who is dealing with pornography addiction as well as other sexual addictions. On that site, an article entitled "Help for Struggling Christian Leaders" states:

"Online pornography consumption is a growing concern among clergy. Almost one of every seven calls received on the Focus on the Family Pastoral Care Line is regarding

Internet pornography. Some pastors are just dabbling, others are headed towards addiction, and some are crying for help as they try to break free from the addiction."[2]

We must be sensitive in our spirits to know what will have a negative effect on us when we see it, and turn it off immediately! In Psalm 101:3 the psalmist wrote, "I will set nothing wicked before my eyes." We need help to do this, so we need to pray: "Turn away my eyes from looking at worthless things, and revive me in Your way" (Psalm 119:37).

Temptation triggered by visual stimuli is an area in which men are especially vulnerable, because God made males to be sexually stimulated by sight. In the book *Every Man's Battle*, Stephen Arterburn and Fred Stoeker talk of "bouncing the eyes" and "starving the eyes." They encourage men to train their eyes to immediately bounce away from an obvious sexual temptation—whether it is a lingerie ad or a female jogger on the side of the road—"like the jerk of your hand away from a hot stove."[3] Sometimes the next step of starving your eyes is necessary. If you know something is a temptation, stay away from it. What good is seeing a movie with a good plot if the sexual scenes cause you to lust? A good rule of thumb is "When in doubt, do without!"

We have addressed what we see when we look out of the window of our soul, but what do people see when they look in? They can oftentimes perceive our attitude. Remember, actions speak louder than words, and our eyes have a lot to do with communication. Have you ever seen someone joke with a person and then turn and wink at another to let them know they are joking? The first person, however, was not aware it was a joke. In this case, the wink of the eye is almost like what kids do when they cross their fingers behind their back to make the lie they are telling OK. We need to be careful that we are not deceiving through our eyes.

We communicate many things with our eyes. Flirtation, accusation, confusion—you name it, we can show just about any emotion with our eyes. Flirtation with the eyes between two people who are married to other spouses can be the first step on the road to divorce. Also, accusing eyes can be dangerous to a relationship. Just think of the saying, "If looks could kill!" Well, such looks *can* kill a relationship.

Most of us have probably not given much thought to how we use our eyes, but we *need* to think about it. In the same way that we need to be sensitive to the Holy Spirit about what we speak with our mouths, we also need to be sensitive about how we "speak" with our eyes. In Proverbs 6:17, a "proud look" is first in the list of the seven things God hates.

As we dig deeper into the well and spend time with God, the pleasures we experience while in His presence will then shine out through our eyes so people will see the light of Christ! We just may have an opportunity to witness with our words when someone who is looking into our eyes, the windows of our soul, sees something different and proclaims, "There is just something different about you. What is it?"

Going Deeper

Using Our Eyes in the Wrong Way

"The lamp of the body is the eye. If therefore your eye is good, your whole body will be full of light. [23] But if your eye is bad, your whole body will be full of darkness. If therefore the light that is in you is darkness, how great is that darkness!" Matthew 6:22-23

Judging
Read Matthew 7:1-5. In your own words, what is this saying to you?

Haughtiness
Read Psalm 18:27.
What will God do to the humble?
What will He do to "haughty looks"?

Rebellion

In Proverbs 30:17, what does the eye do to the father?
What does the eye do to the mother?
What a warning! God will not put up with rebellion!

Harmful Winking

In Proverbs 10:10, "He who winks with the eye causes
_____."

In Proverbs 6:12-15, what kind of person "winks with his eye?"
What other things does it say he does?
What will happen to him?

In Proverbs 16:30, what is the purpose of winking?

Flirting

A little bit of flirting for those in the dating stage of life may be all right, but many times flirting is not pleasing to the Lord. Look what God will do to those with flirting eyes according to Isaiah 3:16-17:

Isaiah 3:16 (NIV)

"The Lord says,
'The women of Zion are haughty,
walking along with outstretched necks,
flirting with their eyes,
tripping along with mincing steps,
with ornaments jingling on their ankles.' "
(emphasis added)

Isaiah 3:17 (NKJV)
"Therefore the Lord will strike with a scab
The crown of the head of the daughters of Zion,
And *the Lord will uncover their secret parts.*"
(emphasis added)

Lust/Adultery

According to 1 John 2:16, where does lust of the eyes come from?

Read Matthew 5:27-28. In verse 28, what does Jesus day about anyone who *"looks at a woman lustfully"?*

This might be a hard verse to swallow, but it was spoken by our Lord. Remember, men, the thought that comes with the first look is the temptation, and temptation is not a sin. The sin comes when you take that temptation into your thought life and continue to dwell on it. And as we have said before, with every temptation, God brings a way to escape (1 Corinthians 10:13).

God confirms that we can commit adultery with our eyes:

> "With eyes full of adultery, they never stop sinning; they seduce the unstable; they are experts in greed—an accursed brood!" 2 Peter 2:14

Anyone who has a problem with this needs to do what Job 31:1 says:

> "I made a covenant with my eyes
> not to look lustfully at a girl."

Using Our Eyes in the Right Way

A Cheerful Look

> "A cheerful look brings joy to the heart,
> and good news gives health to the bones." Proverbs 15:30
> (NIV)

According to this verse, what does a "cheerful look" bring?

A Generous Eye

According to Proverbs 22:9, whoever has a "generous eye" will be _____. Why?

Shut Your Eyes to Evil!

Read Isaiah 33:15-17. Shutting eyes to evil is just one of the characteristics describing a person who "walks righteously." What other characteristics are listed?

What will happen to the one who walks righteously?

Keep Your Eyes on the Word!

Read Proverbs 4:20-22. Why are we urged to not let God's words depart from our eyes?

According to Acts 17:11, what did the Bereans do?

We need to make sure we do not believe everything we hear a Bible teacher teach. We need to search the Bible for ourselves to see if what he teaches lines up with scripture.

Keep Your Eyes on the Lord!

Write out Psalm 25:15.

Prayer

Father, I desire to live a pure life. I realize that what I do with my eyes will either hinder or promote that desire. Please help me in this area with my eyes. Show me situations in which I use my eyes in ways that are not pleasing to You so that I may confess my sins and receive Your help in overcoming them. I pray that when people look into my eyes, they will be able to see Your light shining forth! In Jesus' Name! Amen!

The Sense of Sight

Day 3

Demonic Deception: A Veil Over Our Eyes

A s Christians, though we have Jesus in our hearts, sometimes focusing on our circumstances, instead of on God's promises, hinders us from seeing God in the midst of those circumstances. I once taught a group of senior citizens in a nursing home, and I illustrated this point by making a red heart out of construction paper and decorating it with a face and hair bow. I said something like, "This is Merry Heart. She has a smile on her face because she has Jesus in her heart, and He brings her joy. However, one day Merry got upset at the nurse for not coming right when she called for her." When I said that, I threw a rag on top of the heart. Then I said, "The next day Merry started thinking of her son's family and wondered why they were not coming to visit." Another rag was thrown on the heart. I continued coming up with things that could happen that would add to the clutter. Then I explained, "Satan wants to rob you of your joy. He will do anything he can to dump clutter on your heart, but if you look to the Lord, He'll take the clutter off and you can have your joy back!" I then proclaimed truths from God's Word and began shaking off the rags to reveal the smile on Merry's face. As I did, I began to see smiles on their faces!

Scripture tells in 2 Corinthians 3:15-18 of Jews having a veil over their hearts concerning the Messiah, but we all allow veils to cover our hearts when we let the cares of this world occupy our attention. So this scripture applies to us: "But even to this day, when Moses is read, a veil lies on their heart. [16] Nevertheless when one turns to the Lord, the veil is taken away. [17] Now the Lord is the Spirit; and where the Spirit of the Lord is, there is liberty. [18] But we all, with unveiled face, beholding as in a mirror the glory of the Lord, are being transformed into the same image from glory to glory, just as by the Spirit of the Lord."

The enemy loves to bring confusion, accusations, misunderstanding, gossip, fear and anxiety. These are all veils over the eyes of our hearts. The moment we take our eyes off God, these things begin to veil our hearts. This is when strife and division can establish a foothold. Strife and division in a church lead to church splits and stunted growth. Between individuals, strife leads to broken relationships. Unity happens when each one looks to God and allows Him to reveal His perspective.

On Day 5 of "Sight" we will be talking about how we all have a threefold purpose—that is, to love God and get to know Him, to love each other in the body of Christ, and to love the people in the world by sharing the Gospel with them. Satan and all his demonic forces work to see that Christians are distracted in each of these areas. The forces of the enemy are especially concerned with hindering the time we spend getting to know God, because God is love. When we make time in our busy schedules to be with God, He teaches us how to truly love. When we love each other in the body of Christ, we will be more effective in reaching out to the lost in our community and beyond. When we love the people in the world, doors of evangelism will start opening for us to share the light of the glorious Gospel with them.

What is evangelism? In *The Complete Book of Everyday Christianity,* Robert Banks and R. Paul Stevens explain evangelism:

> "One of the terms used most frequently in the New Testament to describe the Christian message is the Greek word *euangelion*, which means 'good news.' The English word *evangelism* is derived from that and simply means 'sharing the good news.' When Jesus visited the synagogue in his home village of Nazareth, he declared, quoting from the Old Testament book of Isaiah, that his purpose was 'to bring good news to the poor ... to proclaim release to the captives and recovery

of sight to the blind, to let the oppressed go free, to proclaim the year of the Lord's favor' (Luke 4:18-19 NRSV)."[1]

Of course there are two sides to evangelism—the person sharing the Gospel and the person receiving the Gospel. Satan works at deceiving both sides. If he succeeds in hindering the Christian, he then keeps the seed of the Gospel from ever being planted. If he is not successful with that, he will then try to blind the one receiving the Gospel message. If he succeeds with that, he steals the seed after it has been planted. The Bible tells us that Jesus came to bring "recovery of sight to the blind." Of course we know this refers to the physical healing of blind eyes to see, but it also means that He heals the spiritually blind. He rips off the veil that Satan has placed on them so that they will clearly see the choice He has laid before them of life and death (Deuteronomy 30:19).

2 Corinthians 4:3-6: "But even if our gospel is veiled, it is veiled to those who are perishing, [4] whose minds the god of this age has blinded, who do not believe, lest the light of the gospel of the glory of Christ, who is the image of God, should shine on them. [5] For we do not preach ourselves, but Christ Jesus the Lord, and ourselves your bondservants for Jesus' sake. [6] For it is the God who commanded light to shine out of darkness, who has shone in our hearts to give the light of the knowledge of the glory of God in the face of Jesus Christ."

The most obvious way the enemy keeps the people in the world in darkness is to get them to believe that the most important priority is to look out for "number 1,"—that is self. Remember that sin is "Self Indulgent Nature." People are urged to feed that sin nature everywhere they turn. The attitude is "I deserve it!" As long as "self" is the central focus, God cannot be the Lord of a person's life.

This problem of keeping self the top priority leads to holding on to the offenses we allow ourselves to receive from others. When that happens, envy and hate grow, and the darkness that John wrote about in 1 John 2:9-11 continues: "He who says he is in the light, and hates his brother, is in darkness until now. [10] He who loves his brother abides in the light, and there is no cause for stumbling in him. [11] But he who hates his brother is in darkness and walks in darkness, and does not know where he is going, because the darkness has blinded his eyes."

It is time to bring light to the dark world! We need to pray that God will remove the veil that Satan has tried to put over our eyes to keep us from taking God's light to the darkness. We then need to pray that God will remove the veil from those whom Satan has blinded so that they will be able to receive our message. As His Word tells us in 1 John 1:5: "This is the message which we have heard from Him and declare to you, that God is light and in Him is no darkness at all."

Going Deeper

Who is Satan?
Read the following scriptures, write how each verse refers to Satan, and answer the questions:

John 8:44 -
> What does it say about what Satan says?

John 14:30 -
> What does Jesus say about Satan?

2 Corinthians 4:4 -
> What does it say Satan has done?

Ephesians 2:2 -
> In whom does Satan work?

2 Timothy 2:26 –
> What does Satan do to us before we come to our senses and escape his snare?

1 Peter 5:8 -
> What does it say Satan does?
> What does it say we should do?

Revelation 12:9-10 –
> Verse 9 says that he _____ the whole
world.

> *(Note: Deception is of the enemy. We need to be careful that we
> do not ever try to twist the truth with the intention of deceiving
> anyone. That is where the saying "pull the wool over their eyes"
> comes from. It means to deceive. Remember, Satan puts a veil
> over people's eyes. We do not want to have anything to do with
> that—even in a business deal!)*

> Verse 10 says that he _____ the brethren.

> Good news! What does this passage say will happen to him?

Other Things Satan Does
Read Luke 13:10-17. In verse 16, what did Jesus say Satan had
done to the woman before Jesus freed her?

Read Matthew 4:1-11. In verse 1, who led Jesus to the wilder-
ness and why?
How did Jesus respond to Satan's temptations?
What happened after Satan gave up?

You may also want to read about the parable of the seed and the
sower in Matthew 13:3-8,18-23 and the parable of the wheat and the
tares in Matthew 13:24-30,37-43 to see what role the devil plays in
these parables. If you do, consider journaling about what God shows
you as you read these verses.

Jesus Came to Destroy Satan

After Satan succeeded in deceiving Eve to sin, God prophesied to him in Genesis 3:15. Write that verse out:

The "Seed of the woman" is Jesus. This is the first prophesy about the coming Messiah. The word for "head" is also used for rank or position of headship. In between the time Jesus died on the cross and when He rose triumphantly on the third day, He went down to Hell and took the keys of death, hell and the grave! When He did that, He crushed Satan's headship or authority! Praise God that when we make Him the Lord of our life, Satan is also under our feet! Jesus has already won the victory for us so we do not have to try to win the victory ourselves. When we have trials, we are called to join in the triumph of the victory that Jesus has already won!

1 John 3:8 reiterates Jesus' purpose for coming to Earth. What was it?

Read Hebrews 2:14-15. When Jesus destroys the power of the devil in us, what does He deliver us from?

How does that make you feel?

What Can We Do?

We are not ignorant of Satan's devices, according to 2 Corinthians 2:11. To find out the context, read verses 10 and 11. What do we need to do so that Satan will not take advantage of us?

Satan does not want you to forgive because if you do not forgive, the person you are hurting is yourself. Unforgiveness is one of the biggest hindrances to intimacy with God. You cannot bless God and curse your brother at the same time! (See James 3:9-11and Mark 11:25.)

Read 2 Corinthians 10:3-5. List what you think are the "weapons of our warfare."

Read Ephesians 6:10-18 and list the parts of the armor of God with which we need to be clothed as we are in spiritual battles.

That is what I call protection!

Prayer

Write out your own prayer in response to what you have learned today, and then pray the "Spiritual Warfare Prayer."

Spiritual Warfare Prayer

Thank You, Lord, for placing the **Helmet of Salvation** on my head. It will protect me against any thought-bomb the enemy tries to place in my mind. I will not take them on as my thoughts in the name of Jesus! I place my thoughts in Your hands. Please forgive me for the thoughts I hold on to that are not of You. I ask You to change my mindset to be more like the mind of Christ. Thank You for transforming me by the renewing of my mind.

Thank You, Lord, for placing the **Breastplate of Righteousness** on me. It will protect my heart. Lord, I place all my emotions in Your hands. Help me to remember that You are with me regardless of whether I feel it or not. Please forgive me when I fear. Thank You that though my righteousness is as filthy rags, yet You have clothed me with Your righteousness because of what You did at Calvary!

Thank You, Lord, for placing the **Belt of Truth** on my waist. Please reveal any hindrance or lie I have been holding on to that would keep me from trusting You and replace it with Your Truth, oh Lord! Help me to let go of my perspective of the Truth and seek Your perspective, knowing that Your Truth will set me free! Help me also to have a deaf ear to the lies of Satan and give me ears to hear what the Spirit says.

Thank You, Lord, that my feet are shod with the **Preparation of the Gospel of Peace.** I am being prepared for the calling of God on my life to take the Gospel of Peace to others. Help me to remember that no matter what I go through, You will use the circumstances in my life, both good and bad, to prepare me for the destiny You have chosen for me. Thus I can have peace in the midst of the storm. Thank You that every step I take will be in Peace and that I can take that Peace to people wherever I go!

Thank You, Lord, for putting within my hand the **Shield of Faith,** whereby I can quench every fiery dart of the wicked one. Help me to remember that faith is the substance of things hoped for, the evidence of things not seen and that without faith it is impossible to please You. Forgive me when I have gone forward in my own strength and abilities instead of totally relying on You. Help me to dwell in the Secret Place of the Most High where I will be protected from any onslaught of the enemy.

Thank You, Lord, for giving me the **Sword of the Spirit, which is the Word of God** — the only offensive weapon. All the other armor You give me is for protection, and I thank You for just how protected I really am! This weapon is the only thing I need to combat the enemy. It is really an arsenal of many weapons that are not carnal, but are mighty through God to the pulling down of strongholds. Forgive me when I fail to read and study Your Word when You have prompted me to do so. I choose to read Your Word, meditate on Your Word, memorize Your Word and use Your Word against the enemy in due time. Help me to not fret over what I will say, but to trust Your Spirit to give me just the right Word in the very hour I need it. I do not want to debate Your Word thereby casting pearls before swine, but I will speak Your Word to those who are hungry for it as well as proclaim to the enemy "It is Written!" Remind me also, that my enemy is not flesh and blood — it is not any person, including myself — but it is Satan and all the principalities with him. Therefore, I pray that You would remind me to not let corrupt communication proceed out of my mouth but that which is good to the use of edifying, that it may minister grace unto the hearers.

And having done all, I will stand! Thank You that the battle is not mine, but it is Yours! Thank You for the victory in Christ Jesus who came to destroy the works of the enemy! In reality, the enemy has already been crushed under Your feet by your death and resurrection. He is therefore under my feet as I trust in You and let You dwell in me! I am more than a conqueror through You who love me with a perfect love that casts out all fear! And for that I will ever be grateful!

The Sense of Sight

Day 4

Where is Your Focus?

God has created each of us with a unique purpose and destiny to positively influence the world around us. He has also placed within each of us abilities and desires to walk out that destiny. In other words, the dreams He has given you *are* within your reach with His help, or He would have never given them to you. God is not about dangling a carrot in front of your face that you can never reach! However, sometimes the dreams we have are not really God-given and thus may not come to fruition. Ephesians 2:10 says, "For we are His workmanship, created in Christ Jesus for good works, which God prepared beforehand that we should walk in them." We need to pray for discernment to know which ideas are what He planned beforehand that we should fulfill. We can plan to do many "good" things for God and for others, but if they are not "God assignments" for us, we will be spinning our wheels.

The dreams that are from God are not fulfilled without a price. Before we see our dreams become reality, we will experience some testing along the way. Jesus let us know in John 16:33 that we would have trials: "These things I have spoken to you, that in Me you may have peace. In the world *you will have tribulation*; but be of good cheer, I have overcome the world." (Emphasis added.)

Our natural tendency when we go through hard times is to lose focus. Our mind runs away with us, and our thoughts are centered on the negatives: the "what ifs" and the "if onlys." When that happens, we lose our joy. The Bible says that for the *joy* set before Him, Jesus endured the cross. When I was a child, I learned an acrostic for "joy" in children's church:

Jesus
Others
You

I was taught that in order to have joy, you have to put Jesus first, others second and yourself last. What I would like to propose is that if you have the right *focus* on Jesus, others and yourself during trials, you will keep your JOY!

I. Focus on **Jesus**

Jesus has always been and always will be!

> "In the beginning was the Word, and the Word was with God, and the Word was God. [2] He was in the beginning with God. [3] All things were made through Him, and without Him nothing was made that was made. [4] In Him was life, and the life was the light of men. [5] And the light shines in the darkness, and the darkness did not comprehend it." John 1:1-5

He is the Light of the World. When we go through a trial and forget that truth, we will be in the darkness, not even realizing that the Lord is with us.

God is Faithful!

> "No temptation has overtaken you except such as is common to man; but God is faithful, who will not allow you to be tempted beyond what you are able, but with the temptation will also make the way of escape, that you may be able to bear it." 1 Corinthians 10:13

Remember, with every trial comes the temptation to lose your focus! You may be tempted to do many things: give up, turn to alcohol or nicotine, show your frustration in a fit of rage. The list goes on and on, but the bottom line is that underlying each of these temptations is the temptation to lose focus and not look to Jesus to see us through.

God is with us!

"When you pass through the waters,
I will be with you;
and when you pass through the rivers,
they will not sweep over you.
When you walk through the fire,
you will not be burned;
the flames will not set you ablaze." Isaiah 43:2

II. Focus on **Others**

We are not the only ones affected by our trial!

When we go through a trial, we sometimes lose focus that *other people beside ourselves are affected by our trial.* As a mother, I know that my daughters pick up very quickly on when I am stressed. That truth alone should remind us to get out of the self-pity mode and serve those around us in love. The enemy would love for us to believe that no one else is affected by our trials, because no one else cares about us. The truth is that God has placed each of us, whether we are married, single or divorced, with friends and family who all need each other.

Forgiveness is vitally important!

In most cases, not only are other people affected, but usually the trial will also involve someone whom you need to forgive. Many trials are caused because people hurt each other—whether they mean to or not. Look at Jesus and see how He handled his trials. He was despised and rejected of men, like a lamb led to the slaughter, but He opened not His mouth (Isaiah 53:3,7). Peter also reminds us in 1 Peter 2:21-23, "For to this you were called, because Christ also suffered for us, leaving us an example, that you should follow His steps: [22] 'Who committed no sin, nor was deceit found in His mouth'; [23] who, when He was reviled, did not revile in return; when He suffered, He did not threaten, but committed Himself to Him who judges righteously."

Even after Jesus had been nailed to the cross, He proclaimed in Luke 23:34, "Father, forgive them, for they know not what they do!" We need to remember two things that make forgiveness easier and show us that forgiving is not an option, but a mandate:

1.) **We do not wrestle against flesh and blood**.

"For we do not wrestle against flesh and blood, but against principalities, against powers, against the rulers of the darkness of this age, against spiritual hosts of wickedness in the heavenly places" (Ephesians 6:12). If we remember this, it enables us to forgive more easily because we know that people are not the enemy. Can Christians be used by the enemy? You better believe it! This might be shocking news to you, but we have all been used by the enemy at one time or another. Sometimes it can be a simple as the enemy twisting our words to sound like something we do not mean before they even get to another person's ears! Other times, Satan feeds us lies about ourselves and others that, when we take his bait and believe those lies, we may make choices that hurt others.

2.) **Since God has forgiven us for so much, we are required by God to forgive others.**

Think about how much forgiveness Christ has shown to us. Because He has granted us such great forgiveness, we must forgive others. "And be kind to one another, tenderhearted, forgiving one another, just as God in Christ forgave you" (Ephesians 4:32). In fact, the Bible tells us that if we do not forgive others, God will not forgive us. (See Matthew 6:14-15 and Mark 11:25-26.)

III. Focus on **You**

Remember, it's not about you!

We have already discussed this in Day 3 of "Touch," but it is worth repeating. The minute we begin to think about ourselves and about all the negative circumstances that have come our way, we forget who will rescue us, and who has rescued us in the past. We do not have to understand everything to be able to trust God. "Trust in the Lord with all your heart; lean not on your own understanding. In all your ways acknowledge Him, and He will direct your paths" (Proverbs 3:5-6).

You need to know up front that if you want to go all the way with Jesus, *it's going to cost something.*

That means that trials will come. If we want to be overcomers, we must have something to overcome! Jesus let His disciples know this: "Remember the word that I said to you, 'A servant is not greater than his master.' If they persecuted Me, they will also persecute you" (John 15:20).

If you embrace the suffering you are going through, you will develop intimacy with God and get to know Him better.

This is true with all types of suffering, and especially if it is for righteousness' sake. And it's true whether the persecution is from the world (for example, the loss of a business deal because you would not lie when your boss wanted you to bend the rules just this once to land the deal) or from brothers and sisters in the body of Christ (such as when you are sincerely trying to live for Christ and minister where you have been placed and people misunderstand your actions or judge you unfairly). Paul said in Philippians 3:10 that we can know Him in the fellowship of His sufferings! If everything in our lives were always easy, we would not develop such a dependence on God. We would also not have opportunities to learn lessons in the school of hard knocks.

One of the things God might want us to learn when someone is critical of us is that there might be some truth to what they are saying about us. In that case, we can benefit from criticism if we heed it. Proverbs tells us that a wise man will receive criticism. We need to take what is said about us to God and ask Him to show us if it was spoken in truth (so we can heed it and be refined), or if it was spoken out of deception or woundedness (so we can let it go). Either way, we run to Him and are released when He shows us His perspective!

God uses the trials in our lives to build our character. When we come through difficulties clinging tightly to Jesus we will bring souls into the kingdom, because we are lifting up Christ, and He said when we do that, He will draw all men unto Him! A direct result of our trials then—*if we let Him use them to make us better, instead of letting the enemy use them to make us bitter*—is that we will in some way have a part in someone coming to Christ! Whether we are the one who leads a person to God in prayer or we just show Jesus to someone and are one of many who help that person make his decision to follow Christ, either way God will use our trials to bring others to Him through us. Is a soul worth what you are going through?

You are special to Him!

You must remember in order to have the right focus on yourself in the midst of a trial. Although it is true that we need to remember "not to think more highly of ourselves than we ought" (Romans 12:3), if we take this admonition to the extreme, it will bring about low self-esteem, which will keep us in a destructive self-pity mode. We then forget that we are indeed special to our Creator. This truth brings us back to God! It is His Spirit that draws us to Him! We can then say, "Jesus, You are the center of my joy!"

Going Deeper

Focus on Jesus

Let's review Hebrews 12:1-2 that we saw in "Going Deeper" of Taste Day 1. In verse 1, what are the two things that the author tells us to lay down?

What do you think are the differences between the two?

Who do we look to in order to lay down our weights and our sins? (Verse 2)

Read Hebrews 13:5 and 1 Chronicles 28:20. What promise can we claim from these verses?

Read Psalm 27:1. To which area of your life does this verse pertain now?

Remember that for the joy set before Him, Christ endured the cross for you! When He looks back at what He did on the cross, He is satisfied!

> Isaiah 53:11 (New Living Translation) – "When he sees all that is accomplished by his anguish, he will be satisfied. And because of what he has experienced, my righteous servant will make it possible for many to be counted righteous, for he will bear all their sins."

Focus on Others

As was mentioned in Day 3 of "Touch," 1 Corinthians 2:10-11 shows us that one of Satan's devices is to keep us harboring bitterness and unforgiveness. How do you know if you have truly forgiven someone? When you can do what is listed in 1 Peter 3:8-9. What does that passage tell us to do?

Take some time right now to pray and ask God if there is anyone you need to forgive. You may want to journal a prayer of forgiveness and blessing for them. *Unforgiveness will block God's blessings in our lives and hinder us from knowing God intimately.* This could be a day of release for you!

Focus on You

Read Romans 12:3-5 and answer the following questions:

Verse 3 – What does this verse warn us not to do?

Verses 4 and 5 - Why are we not to think too highly of ourselves?

According to Romans 8:18, what is God's perspective on suffering?

You are special to God! Read 1 John 4:10-16. How do you know God loves you?

Take a moment to write down an example of a time (or times) God let you know how special you are to Him. You may want to include scriptures that ministered to you.

Prayer

Dear Lord, please forgive me for the times when I get distracted with all that is going on in my life and I lose my focus. Thank You that in You I can have "joy unspeakable and full of glory" (1 Peter 1:8)! I know that I will be able to keep that joy as long as I keep the right focus on You, others and myself in the midst of trials. I can do that only as I yield to Your Spirit as You work in and through me. Please remind me when I start to lose my focus. Thank You that when I do, I can come running back to You and refocus on Your truth. I choose to seek Your perspective and be set free from the lies of the enemy!

The Sense of Sight

Day 5

Our Vision: A Threefold Purpose

"What could be worse than being born without sight? Being born with sight and no vision." *Helen Keller*

Some people have the wrong concept of Christianity. They think that Christianity is just a list of rules that restrict those who follow them from having any freedom. Au contraire! Jesus said that He came that we might have life and that we might have it more abundantly (John 10:10). People may think they have freedom when they live a lifestyle that allows them to do whatever they want to, whenever they want to do it, in pursuit of satisfying the desires of their five senses. In reality, they are in bondage, because that kind of lifestyle leads to death. As Jesus said in Mark 8:36, "For what will it profit a man if he gains the whole world, and loses his own soul?"

Most people who live like that on the weekends do so because they spend all week monotonously going through their daily routine. They wake up, get ready, go to work, come home, fix dinner, go to bed just to repeat the same routine the next day—a routine that lacks any sense of joy or purpose. Steven Curtis Chapman sings on "More to This Life," "there's more to this life, than living and dying; more than just trying to make it through the day,"[1] and Stacie Orrico muses on "(There's Gotta Be) More to Life": "There's gotta be more to life than chasing down every temporary high to satisfy me." She goes on, "...there's gotta be more than wanting more."[2] If there is not more, then it really does not matter how we live our lives, because there is no set purpose for living. On the other hand, if we were all created with purpose, then there can be excitement as we walk out our day-to-day routine knowing that God will use assignments in our personal day planner to bring about the purposes He has in mind for our lives!

When someone speaks of having a "vision" in life, what are they talking about? Some may mean having a list of goals, or maybe a plan to achieve one's desires to improve his life, business or organization. But "vision" is more than that.

In the King James Version of the Bible, Proverbs 29:18 says, "Where there is no vision, the people perish: but he that keepeth the law, happy is he." The same verse in the New International Version says, "Where there is no revelation, the people cast off restraint; but blessed is he who keeps the law." At first observation, the two versions might seem to have different meanings, but really they are saying the same thing. "Vision" in this verse is "revelation." When one sees something, it is revealed to him. What we are talking about here is divine revelation. When God gives you divine revelation, you will know His desires. Those people who do not acknowledge God in their lives cannot have that divine revelation until they turn to Him. They also "cast off restraint" by living life with what they call "freedom," living any way they choose to satisfy their own selfish desires. This way of living leads to death. God gives us guidelines in His Word not to punish us but to protect us. The next part of the verse states that whoever keeps God's laws is blessed.

We cannot be any more blessed than when God gives us divine revelation! When He does, we will be more aware of the "vision" and purposes He has for our lives. We each have a threefold purpose:

1.) to love God and get to know Him
2.) to love each other in the body of Christ
3.) to love the people in the world by sharing the gospel with them.

Love God and Get to Know Him

God created us to commune with Him. He loved us so much that He created us with a free will so that we would have the choice to serve Him or not. We were not made like robots already programmed to automatically love God. That would not be true love if we had no choice.

The good news is that God, being omniscient or all knowing, knew that man would fall into sin, so He provided a plan so that man could be reconciled to Him. God the Father loved us so much that He sent His Son, Jesus, into the world as a man to pay the price for our redemption.

"In him we have redemption through his blood, the forgiveness of sins, in accordance with the riches of God's grace [8] that he lavished on us with all wisdom and understanding." Ephesians 1:7-8 NIV

The triune God loves us and wants us to be reconciled to Him to have communion with Him as Adam did in the Garden of Eden before sin entered the picture. When we understand that God sent Jesus, that Jesus died for us, and that the Holy Spirit draws us to Him, then we will respond to His love. We will read the Word and spend time in worship and prayer to satisfy the void in our lives that can only be filled by our Creator. As we seek Him, He begins to open our spiritual eyes and give us revelation knowledge that leads to knowing His plans for our lives.

"...that the God of our Lord Jesus Christ, the Father of glory, may give to you the spirit of wisdom and revelation in the knowledge of Him, [18] the eyes of your understanding being enlightened; that you may know what is the hope of His calling..." Ephesians 1:17-18

Love Each Other in the Body of Christ

The church is "one body" but "many members." God has plans for the church as His body, as well as unique purposes for each individual in the body. He places people with different gifts and abilities in the body as He pleases so that every need a person has can be met through people in the church. He places passions and desires in each person so that they will want to fulfill the need that He has placed them in the church to meet. As they spend time with Him fulfilling their first purpose, to get to know Him, these passions for ministry to other believers will become evident. As individuals in a church body tap into what Christ, the Head of the Body, wants them to do, the church will grow with new believers, and the members will be edified in love.

> "...the whole body, joined and knit together by what every joint supplies, according to the effective working by which every part does its share, causes growth of the body for the edifying of itself in love." Ephesians 4:16

Unfortunately, this process is often hindered because of strife among believers. There are many factors that can lead to strife in a church. When people in the church judge other people's differences instead of appreciating the diversity that helps meet needs, their critical spirit will hinder the effectiveness of the whole church. Also, when people either do not fulfill their position in the church, or they fulfill the wrong position because someone expects them to instead of God stirring them to do it, strife will fester and the body will be paralyzed. It is time that we wake up!

> "Therefore He says:
> 'Awake, you who sleep,
> Arise from the dead,
> And Christ will give you light.'
> [15] See then that you walk circumspectly, not as fools but as wise, [16] redeeming the time, because the days are evil. [17] Therefore do not be unwise, but understand what the will of the Lord is. [18] And do not be drunk with wine, in which is dissipation; but be filled with the Spirit, [19] speaking to one another in psalms and hymns and spiritual songs, singing and making melody in your heart to the Lord, [20] giving thanks always for all things to God the Father in the name of our Lord Jesus Christ, [21] submitting to one another in the fear of God." Ephesians 5:14-21

When we pursue this path, our churches will be places where wounded soldiers in God's army can come and be healed, and the enlisted can be prepared and encouraged as they are sent to the battle outside the walls of the church! This will prepare members in the body to fulfill the third purpose we each have, to evangelize the world.

Love the People in the World By Sharing the Gospel with Them

As we spend more time getting to know God, we will begin to have His heart for reaching the lost. We begin to want to share in His plan of reconciliation, bringing the lost to a restored relationship with their Creator. What is neat is that He *wants* us to share in the ministry of reconciliation!

> "Now all things are of God, who has reconciled us to Himself through Jesus Christ, and has given us the ministry of reconciliation, [19] that is, that God was in Christ reconciling the world to Himself, not imputing their trespasses to them, and has committed to us the word of reconciliation. [20] Now then, we are ambassadors for Christ, as though God were pleading through us: we implore you on Christ's behalf, be reconciled to God." 2 Corinthians 5:18-20

Today, our world has a population of 6.1 billion people; 4.4 billion, or 73%, are evangelized, leaving 1.7 billion, or 27%, who are not.[3] That means that almost one third of our world has not been reached with the Good News of Jesus Christ. People are dying every minute without God. How tragic! We need to pray and ask God what we can do to help.

We can definitely do more. Prayer is foundational. Jesus said to His disciples in Matthew 9:37-38: "The harvest truly is plentiful, but the laborers are few. [38] Therefore pray the Lord of the harvest to send out laborers into His harvest."

We need to pray for more missionaries, and we need to pray for the missionaries who are already giving their lives to spread the Good News. Too many times we are in our comfortable Western churches thinking about our own lives, and we forget to even pray for the needs of the missionaries and for the lost in those mission fields to be ready to receive the Gospel. As we pray for them, the Lord will let us know what else we can do. He will stir hearts of the intercessors to support missions not only in their prayers, but also in their financial offerings. He will also stir some to go to the mission field themselves. We will then be like Isaiah when he saw the Lord sitting on the throne and the train of His robe filled the temple. After Isaiah saw the Lord, he entered into a time of confession and worship, and he recorded in Isaiah 6:8: "Then I heard the voice of the Lord saying, 'Whom shall I send? And who will go for us?' And I said, 'Here am I. Send me!' "

Going Deeper

What is true freedom?
Before Christ enters our lives, we think we are free to do as we choose. Read Romans 6:20-23 and answer these questions:

Verse 20 – When someone is a slave to sin, what are they free from?

Verse 21 – What does that "freedom" result in?

Verse 22 – When someone is set free from sin, they become slaves of _____.
What does that lead to?
What is the result?
Write out and memorize verse 23.

According to 1 Timothy 2:5-6, who is the Mediator between God and man?
What did He do that allows Him to be our Mediator?

Read Titus 2:14. Why did Jesus give Himself for us?

You may want to read the following scriptures that also deal with Christ's redemption of us, and journal what God stirs in your heart:

Hebrews 9:12   1 Peter 1:18-19   Revelation 5:9

Loving God
Read Deuteronomy 6:5-8.
Write out verse 5.

Read verses 6-8. What does this passage tell us to do in order to teach our children about loving God and His Word?

Read John 14:21-23. Summarize these verses by telling what one will do who loves God, and what God will do for the one who loves Him.

Loving Brothers and Sisters in Christ
Read and underline 1 Peter 1:22.

Read 1 Peter 3:8-9 and answer the following questions.
Verse 8 – We should all be of _____ mind. Name the four things this verse tells us to do:
1.

2.

3.

4.

Verse 9 – What does this verse tell us not to do?
What does it tell us to do?
Why?

Look again at the list of seven things God hates in Proverbs 6:17-19. What is the last thing on the list?

Galatians 6:10: "Therefore, as we have opportunity, let us do good to all, especially to those who are of the household of faith."

Loving the Lost People of the World

Read Luke 14:16-23. In your own words, what does this parable tell you about God's heart and our responsibility in reaching the lost?

Read "The Great Commission" written in Matthew 28:18-20. Is sharing the Gospel an option or a command?

We cannot be effective in sharing the Gospel without the power of the Holy Spirit.

> "But you shall receive power when the Holy Spirit has come upon you; and you shall be witnesses to Me in Jerusalem, and in all Judea and Samaria, and to the end of the earth." Acts 1:8

Jerusalem was their community. What is your community?

Judea was the surrounding areas. What are the surrounding areas where you live?

Samaria was nearby, but it was another culture group. Name some culture groups that are prevalent near where you live.

The end of the earth would be foreign lands. Name any countries God may be stirring in your heart or countries where your church has missionaries.

Take time to pray about reaching the lost in each of these areas (your Jerusalem, Judea, Samaria, and the ends of the earth).

Prayer

Lord, I want to see You! I want to know You intimately so that I may know what pleases You. Thank you that according to Ephesians 2:10, I am Your workmanship, created in Christ Jesus for good works, which You prepared beforehand that I should walk in them. I trust that as I spend time getting to know You, You will reveal to me those unique callings that You have especially for me. Help me to not only see the vision of what You are calling me to do in the future, but to also enjoy every step it will take to see that vision carried out. Help me to love as You love and to show that love to my brothers and sisters in the church and to the lost who do not know You. I pray that Your love will enable me to be used to edify the church and reach the lost. In Jesus' precious name, Amen!

The Sense of Hearing

"So then faith comes by hearing, and hearing
by the word of God."
Romans 10:17

Day 1

Hearing: Sound Waves and Good Vibrations

Like the other senses God has given us, our sense of hearing allows us to enjoy the world around us. For instance, we may enjoy a movie so much more because the music sets the mood. Our sense of hearing can also warn us of danger. We run for safety if we hear gunshots or thunder. Unlike the other three senses we have discussed so far, the sense of hearing allows us to know what is around the corner.

The ear is made up of three parts: the outer ear, the middle ear and the inner ear. The outer ear, called the pinna, is the part of the ear that we see. The cartilage in the ear and the folds of skin are shaped perfectly to be able to collect sounds and funnel them through the ear canal to the middle ear. The sounds are actually vibrations in the air called sound waves. The faster the sound waves vibrate, the higher the pitch. As the sound waves reach the middle ear they cause the eardrum to vibrate.

The middle ear, located within a small air-filled cavity of the skull, consists of the eardrum and the three smallest bones of the body called ossicles. There is also a tube called the eustachian tube that runs to the back of the nasal cavity and mouth. The eustachian tube allows air pressure to be adjusted so that it is the same on both sides of the eardrum. We are especially aware of this when we change altitudes, and the air pressure changes. Yawning or swallowing can allow air through the eustachian tube to equalize the air pressure in the ear to match the pressure we feel on the outside.

The eardrum is a thin but tough membrane. The energy of the sound waves causing the eardrum to vibrate becomes stronger as the sound waves are sent through the ossicles that are kept in place with tendons. These three bones are levers that carry the sound and are named for their shape. The first one, which is connected to the eardrum, is the "malleus," also known as the hammer. After traveling through the hammer, the sound waves go through the "incus," also known as the anvil. The next bone to receive the signals is the "stapes," or stirrup. At the end of the stirrup is another drum-like membrane called the oval window that is set on the lining of the inner ear. The vibration of the oval window is sent to the cochlea.

The cochlea (Greek for snail) is a tube that is covered by a tiny layer of bone and wrapped around a tiny central bone in the shape of a snail. Within the cochlea are fluids and tiny hair cells. The vibration of the oval window causes the fluids in the cochlea to move. When the fluids move, the hair cells also move. The hair cells are receptor cells that translate the vibrations into nerve impulses that are then sent to the brain via the cochlear nerve. The impulses are taken to a place in the middle of the brain called the cochlear nucleus. From there, nerve fibers divide into two pathways—one pathway takes the impulses to the left side of the brain, and the other takes them to the right side of the brain. As a result, each hemisphere of the brain receives stimuli from both ears.

The brain sorts through our memories to find the sound that is being heard and lets us know what we are hearing. For example, when a child first hears an ice cream truck bell, they are told what it is. Later, when the child is older and hears the bell again, the brain receives the signal, compares it to other ringing tones that have been heard before and remembers it was an ice cream truck bell rather than a telephone ring or a doorbell.

The brain also screens the messages received from the sound impulses. When we are asleep, there are many sounds, but the brain will "tune them out" so we can sleep. However, if it is something that we need to wake up for, the brain will allow us to be woken up with the sound. This is why a mother can sleep through the sound of rain hitting the roof or an airplane flying over the house, but will wake up at the first sound of her baby's cry.

The brain takes the information from both ears and processes it to tell us not only what it is we are hearing, but also where the sound is coming from. For example, when a sound comes from a person's left side, the sound in the left ear reaches the brain a fraction of a second earlier than the right ear. The sound from the left ear is also slightly louder than the sound from the right ear. When this happens, the brain lets us know that the sound is coming from the left side.

The ear not only allows us to process sound waves, but it also helps us with balance, or equilibrium. Nerve impulses that deal with balance are generated in the semicircular canals located within the inner ear next to the cochlea. The semicircular canals are made up of three tubes that are set at right angles to each other, like the three sides of the corner of a box. Because of the three-dimensional positioning of these canals, we are able to detect movement up and down, side to side, and tilting from one side to the other. Like the cochlea, the semicircular canals are filled with fluid and sensory hair cells. When we move, the fluid in the canals sloshes around and causes the hairs to move. The hairs translate the movement into nerve messages that are sent to the brain via the vestibular nerve. The brain then tells the body how to stay balanced. If one spins around and then stops, the liquid inside the canals keeps moving and the hairs continue to send messages to the brain that he is spinning even though he is not. This is what causes one to feel dizzy. The messages sent to the brain through the vestibular nerve help us to stand erect and in balance on two legs, and even walk in a straight line in the dark.

As we have learned, there is more involved with our sense of hearing than merely observing sounds around us. What we hear influences our emotions. For example, we can experience a peace as we take in sounds of birds chirping and water flowing in a stream, or we can experience an adrenaline rush that causes us to take cover as we are warned with sounds of possible danger. With hearing, we also have a sense of direction and balance. What an awesome God we serve who has made us so intricately and given us this incredible gift of hearing!

Spiritually speaking, we need to pray and ask God to help us sort through all the sounds that come to us. He will also help us to tune out all the noise we hear that will hinder our walk with God and actually help us to know where these noises are coming from. Then we will be on our way to experiencing a balanced Christian walk and will hear His voice as He guides us where He wants us to go.

Going Deeper

Direction

Our sense of hearing helps us have a sense of direction. God wants us to have direction in our lives as well.

Read Isaiah 30:21.

God will give us direction if we ask Him. When He does, we must decide whether or not we will obey His direction. Sometimes this direction comes in the form of warnings, as in Hebrews 12:25-29. These warnings may sound harsh, but we are protected if we heed them.

After reading Hebrews 12:25-29, write the warning and the good we will have in the end if we heed it.

Read Psalm 81:11-12 and write what will happen if we do not heed God's warnings.

Sorting the Sounds

As we have learned, sound waves are translated into nerve impulses and sent to the brain. The brain then sorts out the sounds by sifting through our memories to determine the context in which the sound was heard before and comparing it to other sound memories; our brain then tells us what sound is being heard. In the spiritual realm, the Holy Spirit sorts through many things for us and enables us to hear with spiritual ears.

Read John 14:25-26. What did Jesus say the Holy Spirit will do?

Notice that the Holy Spirit brings to remembrance Jesus' Words that have already been heard. It is so important to study the scriptures so that God's Word will already be filed in our brains for the Holy Spirit to use when He wants to remind us of something. There is an answer in God's Word for any trial we will ever face. We need to read the Word, meditate on the Word, memorize the Word and hear the preaching of the Word! Then when we go through a trial, the Holy Spirit will remind us of just the scripture we need to help us endure.

One of the things the brain does when sorting sounds is that it compares sounds that have been previously heard. Read 1 Corinthians 2:13-14. Verse 13 in the NKJV says, "These things we also speak, not in words which man's wisdom teaches but which the Holy Spirit teaches, comparing spiritual things with spiritual." The New International Version of 1 Corinthians 2:13 says, "This is what we speak, not in words taught us by human wisdom but in words taught by the Spirit, expressing spiritual truths in spiritual words." A person who does not know a language, cannot understand when someone else speaks in that language. These spiritual truths originate from God, and God speaks them to us in spiritual words that we as Christians can understand. We can understand them because we have the Holy Spirit living in us. (See 1 Corinthians 2:14.)

Balance

God created us with such an awesome system in the inner ear to keep our equilibrium balanced. He also wants us to be spiritually balanced. Read Ephesians 4:14. What does this verse mention that would cause us to be spiritually dizzy?

171

Doctrine simply means "that which is taught." Many things are taught in the name of Christianity—some truth and some false teaching—but only God's truth will prevail. According to 2 Timothy 4:3-4, what will men do who do not want to hear sound doctrine?

God wants us to be balanced. When we are spiritually balanced, we will be steadfast. Colossians 1:21-23 talks about us being reconciled to God through Christ's death and presented holy, blameless and above reproach in His sight. What is the condition mentioned in verse 23 that we need meet in order for that to happen?

Prayer

Father, I thank You for the gift of hearing. It is awesome how You fashioned even the cartilage and the folds of the skin in the outer ear to be just the right shape to funnel sounds into the middle ear. And the way very tiny bones work like levers to take the sound waves through the middle ear to the inner ear is incredible! It boggles my mind to think how little hair cells can translate sound waves and motions into nerve impulses to be sent to the brain to identify sounds and tell what to do to stay balanced. Just knowing the way the ear is formed reminds me of You, oh Lord. Thank You that the One who formed my ears is also the One who hears me even now! ("He who planted the ear, shall He not hear? He who formed the eye, shall He not see?" Psalm 94:9) Help me also to hear Your voice and heed Your direction. Thank You for bringing balance to my life. Thank You also for bringing to my remembrance scriptures in the midst of trials. Help me to continue in faith, remain grounded and steadfast, and never move away from the hope of the gospel in Jesus' Name, AMEN!

The Sense of Hearing

Day 2

Misuse Hinders Our Faith

Many of the things we hear have the potential of stunting our spiritual growth if we choose to listen to them. Most of the time, we have a choice whether to allow ourselves to be in a place to hear them or not. As Christians, we should not listen to gossip, coarse jesting or vulgar language. No matter what the style of music, if the lyrics go against God's standard, we need to turn off the radio! We certainly should not have anything to do with hearing anything associated with the occult, such as consulting a psychic about our lives or what they "hear" the dead say (Deuteronomy 18:14). All of these are contrary to God's very character.

The way we misuse our sense of hearing that keeps us from having faith is listening to too many voices instead of concentrating on God's Word. The Bible tells us in Romans 10:17 that "faith comes by hearing, and hearing by the word of God." We hear many sounds in life, but it is only God's Word that brings faith. Hearing words that do not line up with God's Word can lead to fear, deception, anger, depression and anything else that hinders our faith in God.

As we learned in Day 1 of "Hearing," the brain sorts through the sounds we hear and blocks out sounds that are not important. If it didn't, we would be bombarded by so many "voices" vying for our attention that it would drive us crazy. We need to let God sort through the sounds we hear and block out the voices that will not draw us closer to Him. Voices come from four different sources: 1.) self 2.) other people 3.) the devil 4.) God. The first two sources, self and other people, can be used for Satan's agenda, to steal, kill and destroy, or God's agenda, to give us life more abundantly.

Many people joke about talking to themselves. One time when I was eating breakfast with my father-in-law at a restaurant, we witnessed a waitress mumbling to herself the whole time we were there. Most of her comments were about how much she hated her job. At one point she was clearing dishes from a table and said, "How dare they not leave me a good tip when I worked so hard for them!" She kept saying other derogatory things about the customers. My father-in-law and I were laughing as we watched, but really it was not funny; it was sad! She was speaking bitterness into her life that would chase joy a mile a way! She was doing what the psalmist wrote in Psalm 64:5. "They encourage themselves in an evil matter; They talk of laying snares secretly; They say, 'Who will see them?'" This might refer to a group of people—a street gang for instance—who devise criminal schemes. But this waitress did not need anyone else to encourage her in evil; she was doing it to herself! She was speaking negative words over herself and others, which leads to living a defeated life!

It is much better when we speak words to ourselves that will encourage us to be overcomers! The book of 1 Samuel tells us about David doing just that: "Now David was greatly distressed, for the people spoke of stoning him... But David strengthened himself in the Lord his God" 1 Samuel 30:6. There are times when no one will be around to give us words of encouragement. We must learn to "strengthen ourselves in the Lord."

When there *are* others around to speak to us, we need to ask God to help us sort through the things we are hearing. Voices that come from others can either be a hindrance or an aid to our spiritual walk. We already learned in Day 3 of "Taste" that the Hebrew word-picture for "words" is arrows. In ages preceding ours when bows and arrows were the "high-tech" weapons, often times the arrows were laced with poison so that when a person was hit with the arrow, if the arrow did not kill him, the poison would. When someone says something that harms us, we need to go to God and let Him take the arrow out before the poison kills us. Too many times, instead of letting God rescue us, we hold on to the arrow or the poison it carries by continuing to talk about it or dwell on it. "All we hear are the taunts of our mockers. All we see are our vengeful enemies" (Psalm 44:16).

Arrows are not always used for evil. I have seen television documentaries about wild animals in which the people shooting the arrows at the animals were not trying to kill their target, but they were trying to help. The arrow had a tranquilizer on it to put the animal to sleep so that a veterinarian could help the ailing animal or so that a wildlife biologist could put a tracking device on the animal for research. Words that people speak to us also can be used for our good. Paul wrote in Colossians 3:16 how our words can be used in many ways to edify each other: "Let the word of Christ dwell in you richly in all wisdom, teaching and admonishing one another in psalms and hymns and spiritual songs, singing with grace in your hearts to the Lord."

The third source from whom we can hear voices is Satan, who is like "a roaring lion, seeking whom he may devour," (1 Peter 5:8). Satan loves to throw false guilt and condemnation on Christians. Sometimes he tries to make us feel like we were supposed to do something, then if we do not do it, he makes us feel like we missed God, and God will not use us anymore. A friend of mine once told me, "Remember, Tammy, Satan drives, but the Lord leads." Since then I have leaned on that advice when trying to discern if a thought is from the enemy or God. If a thought comes to my mind that I need to do a particular assignment—even if it seems that it would be something for God—I pray to discern if it is from God or not. If I feel pressured and anxious, I realize it is not from God. Does God ever ask us to do something "out of our comfort zone" that we do not want to do? Yes, sometimes He will. However, along with the request comes a gentle leading and an assurance that He will go with us and guide us each step of the way.

The voices of Satan and his demonic hosts have other characteristics. We know that he is the "accuser of the brethren," so when we have thoughts that foster low self-esteem, the source is the enemy. We also have learned that Satan is a deceiver and the father of all lies. He is sneaky. He will make something sound right and be close to the truth, but not completely true. Any thought that is contrary to the Word of God is from the enemy. I once heard about a lady who wanted to be a missionary, but her husband did not hear this call. She said God told her to divorce her husband and leave him and her children to go spread the Gospel in Africa. I can tell you that God did not tell her to do that, because that goes against His Word. Heeding Satan's voice will only lead to confusion, anxiety, fear and death.

God's voice, on the other hand, will bring direction, peace, joy and abundant life! Many people are so worried about hearing God's voice that they miss it when He speaks. For some reason, some people think they need to hear an audible voice from God, and since they do not, they think He does not speak to them. God is Spirit. He dwells within our spirit. The Bible talks of Him having a still, small voice. As we learned in Day 1 of "Hearing," the Holy Spirit will bring things to our remembrance. In other words, He will bring thoughts to our minds. I once heard someone say, "If you have to have an audible voice from God, you are hard of hearing." Prayer needs to be a two-way conversation. Too often we just speak in our prayers, but we do not stop to hear what God has to say to us. He will talk to us; we just need to listen. Jesus said in John 10:27, "My sheep hear My voice, and I know them, and they follow Me."

We also need to remember that God has given us His Word in written form. When we read the Bible and the Holy Spirit quickens something to us, we are hearing from God. As we read the written Word, we are then led by the Spirit to become like Christ, the living Word. As we heed God's Word, we are blessed indeed! *"...blessed are those who hear the word of God and keep it!" Luke 11:28*

Going Deeper

Listening to people

The things we hear people say can either help us or harm us. Read the following verses from Proverbs and write down what the verse mentions is either good or bad to hear and the reason if it is included.

Proverbs 1:8,9 -

Proverbs 1:10,15,16 -

Proverbs 15:1 -

Proverbs 15:4 -

Proverbs 15:5 -

Proverbs 20:19 -

The things that we hear from people that are bad can sometimes cause us to live in fear and anxiety. Psalm 118:8 is the verse that is in the very center of the Bible. It tells us to trust God and not put our confidence in man. Just as all the verses of the Bible center around that verse, our lives should also center on trusting God! Write out and meditate on Psalm 118:6 and 8.

[6] _____

_____

[8] _____

_____

Hearing God's Voice

John 10 speaks of us being the sheep and Jesus being our shepherd. Sheep are known to need guidance. They do, however, know the voice of their shepherd. Read John 10:1-9 and summarize in your own words what this passage is saying to you.

You may also want to read Psalm 23 and write in your journal how the Lord as our Shepherd gently leads us and protects us.

As was mentioned before, many people think they have to hear an audible voice from God. There are only three events recorded in the New Testament when God the Father spoke audibly. Read each of the following passages and tell the event at which God spoke audibly and what He said:

Matthew 3:13-17 - Event:
    What did God say?

Luke 9:28-36 - Event:
    What did God say?

John 12:12-30 - Event:
    What did God say?

Read Hebrews 1:1-2. God speaks to us by _____.
The key to hearing God is getting to know Jesus.

What did Jesus say in John 14:23?

Read John 8:47 *(preferably in the NIV)*. What does the first sentence say?

When God makes His home in us, He will speak to us, and we will hear Him because we are His!

Prayer

Lord, I pray that You would remind me to guard the gate of my ears. I want to hear Your still small voice when You tell me not to listen to something that is not pleasing to You. I pray that You would sort through the sounds that I hear each day, and let me know what is of You and what I need to dismiss. Forgive me for the times that I have talked negatively to others or myself. Forgive me for any time I heeded the voice of the enemy instead of listening to You. Thank You for being my Shepherd. I want to get to know You more, so that I will recognize Your voice more quickly. Thank You for the times You have spoken to me through Your Word.

The Sense of Hearing

Day 3

Hearing Must Lead to Doing!

I remember as a student sitting in science class and being taught that if a tree fell in the forest and there was no one there to hear it, it would not make a sound. The reasoning was that for sound to happen, there not only has to be a source of the sound, but there also has to be a receptor to pick up and process the sound waves. I sat there thinking of all the reasons why I did not believe that. Ultimately, even if all creatures with ears were absent, God would still be there to hear it!

Even though I do not go along with this scientific theory, it is true that if a person hears something, but he does not pay attention to it, then it will not make any difference in his life. Anyone who is a parent knows that children have "selective hearing." If I ask our daughter why she did not clean her room after I asked her to, she will usually say, "Oh, I forgot!" On the other hand, if I tell her we are going to Disney World next month, she'll ask each day, "How long until we get to go to Disney World?"

It is recorded in the gospels six times that Jesus said, "He who has ears to hear, let him hear!" Many were there hearing Him, but not everyone was actually receiving what He was saying. Unless the Spirit is drawing a person, he will not receive the Gospel message that is preached to Him. When the Spirit stirs Him, and he starts taking interest in the message, then he will hear with the kind of hearing that brings about faith.

Jesus often taught truths by telling parables, or stories that apply a principle to everyday life. The parable of the farmer and the seed is all about hearing:

> Luke 8:4-8, 11-15: "While a large crowd was gathering and people were coming to Jesus from town after town, he told this parable: [5] 'A farmer went out to sow his seed. As he was scattering the seed, some fell along the path; it was trampled on, and the birds of the air ate it up. [6] Some fell on rock, and when it came up, the plants withered because they had no moisture. [7] Other seed fell among thorns, which grew up with it and choked the plants. [8] Still other seed fell on good soil. It came up and yielded a crop, a hundred times more than was sown.' When he said this, he called out, 'He who has ears to hear, let him hear. [11] This is the meaning of the parable: The seed is the word of God. [12] Those along the path are the ones who hear, and then the devil comes and takes away the word from their hearts, so that they may not believe and be saved. [13] Those on the rock are the ones who receive the word with joy when they hear it, but they have no root. They believe for a while, but in the time of testing they fall away. [14] The seed that fell among thorns stands for those who hear, but as they go on their way they are choked by life's worries, riches and pleasures, and they do not mature. [15] But the seed on good soil stands for those with a noble and good heart, who hear the word, retain it, and by persevering produce a crop.' "

As I meditated on this parable, I pictured a field that is plowed to prepare the land for planting. When seeds are sown in the plowed ground, some of the seeds fall to the side of the plowed row where the ground is still hard. Before I tell anyone about the great news of Jesus Christ—whether I'm speaking to a group or witnessing to one person—I pray that the Holy Spirit will till the soil of their hearts, so that the seed of the Word of God will fall on good ground.

We also need to pray that all the rocks, or obstacles, will be removed in a person's life that would keep the seed from taking root. This parable tells us that the seed that falls on the rock represents those who receive the word with joy, but have no root. They believe for a while, but then they fall away when trials come. We need to stand by new believers and disciple them. The Christian walk is a process. We cannot just lead someone in a prayer and then forget about him. True discipleship is walking with him and encouraging him along the way. He needs to know that God will take him through the trials that surely will come, and that he will be stronger when each trial is over.

The third example is the seed that fell among thorns and is choked out by the cares of this world. This could mean that desires for material possessions, partying and carousing, etc. take priority over desire for more of God in a person's life. It could also mean that if one cares about what the world cares about more than what God cares about, His Word will be choked out in his life. Many Christians tend to fall into this category from time to time, and they do not even realize it. (See Matthew 6:24-34 for a good comparison about what the world cares about and what God cares about.) We need to pray that the one who receives the Word will develop a deep hunger for more of the Word, so the cares of this world will not even compare to having God in his life!

The seed that falls on good soil produces a crop! We need to pray that the one who hears the message will receive the Word, understand the Word and spread the Word. If we truly receive the Word and apply it to our lives, we will share it with others. We will be like Peter and John in Acts, chapter 4. When they got in trouble for teaching about Jesus, they replied: "Judge for yourselves whether it is right in God's sight to obey you rather than God. For we cannot help speaking about what we have seen and heard" (Acts 4:19).

Going Deeper

True Listening

There is a difference between hearing and listening. When I think of hearing, I think of detecting sounds through the ears. When I think of listening, I think of paying close attention to what is being heard.

Read Acts 16:14-15. The NIV Bible uses "listening" instead of "hearing." While Lydia was listening to the Gospel being preached, what did God do for her?

Notice in verse 15 that after she heard, her whole family was baptized and she practiced hospitality. When one truly listens to the Word and applies it to his life, his works will match up to his profession of faith.

What does Romans 2:13 say?

Read Nehemiah 8:1-12 and answer the following questions:
Verse 1 – What indicates that the people were in unity?

What indicates that the people wanted to hear the scriptures?

Verse 2 – The crowd included:

Verse 3 – How long did Ezra read the scriptures to the people?
What is the last statement of verse 3?

Verse 6 – What was the response of the people to the reading of the scriptures and Ezra
blessing God?

Verses 7 & 8 – What did Ezra's helpers do?

Verse 12 – Why did the people rejoice greatly?

Faith Versus Works
Read, underline, and memorize Ephesians 2:8-9 and James 2:17.

It may seem that what Paul wrote in Ephesians 2:8-9 contradicts with what James wrote in James 2:17, but when we truly understand the role of faith and works, we realize that it is not a contradiction. In the box below, draw a tree with the roots below the line and the trunk, limbs, leaves and fruit above the line. Label the roots "Faith." Label the leaves/fruit "Good Works."

We are not saved by faith <u>and</u> works; rather we are saved by faith <u>that</u> works. ***With knowledge comes responsibility. As we grow in the Lord, we will want to obey His Word, because we will desire to please Him.***

Read Matthew 7:24-27. What did Jesus say about one who hears His words and does them?

What does Jesus say about one who hears his word and does <u>not</u> obey them?

Note: The house had to be built before the storm came. We cannot wait until a storm comes to try to do what God wants us to do.

Prayer

Dear Heavenly Father, I do not want to just hear Your Word, but I want to listen attentively and apply it to my life. I pray that You would till the soil of my heart before I read the Word or hear it being taught. Thank You for the people You are going to put in my path who do not know You. I pray, Holy Spirit, that You would till the soil of their hearts so that they will be ready to receive the seed of the Word of God. When they are ready, I pray I will be bold enough to speak the words that You quicken to me. I pray that all the rocks or obstacles in their lives would be removed so that roots will develop. I pray that they will be so hungry for Your Word that the cares of this world will not compare to what they can have in You. I pray that they will receive the Word, understand the Word and spread the Word! In Jesus' Name, Amen

The Sense of Hearing

Day 4

Close Your Eyes and Open Your Ears!

When I was a music major in college, I was instructed by my trumpet professor to memorize a piece of music and then sit in a dark room with the lights off to practice it. It was then that I stopped just playing the notes, and I made music. I had seen the written music first, and had spent hours with it before my eyes when I was learning it. I drilled the notes measure by measure until I could put it all together. But there came a time when the music itself was a distraction. I played all the printed notes, but I did not play it musically until I closed my eyes to those printed notes, let them become a part of me, and played them with feeling. Finally the crescendos and the decrescendos shaped the phrases; the accents and soft tones of the articulation were in just the right places, and the emotion that the composer hoped the song would convey came through me and out of the brass bell of my trumpet to all who would hear. My trumpet teacher used to say, "Make me cry!"

To hear God, often times you have to close your eyes so you will not be distracted. I am a visionary person. God gives me many dreams and passions that are for long-range assignments. However, sometimes I have to close my eyes to the long-range assignment, or "put it on the back burner" so to speak, so that I will not lose focus on what He wants me to do now. I still know the vision God gave me is there, and in the back of my mind I am still quite excited about it, but I also know there are little steps that are necessary to get to the big dreams.

The enemy will make sure there are other distractions along the way to hinder you from accomplishing those dreams and passions for God. Attacks will come from all directions—finances, health, relationships—the list goes on and on. When they come, you must be determined to focus on God and not on the many distractions.

Sometimes, in your excitement, you may tell the people around you about the exciting vision God has given you, and then the very people you thought would be excited might say something like, "I don't see how you're going to be able to do that." Then the enemy is there ready to throw out his bait so you will take offense at what they have said! Let James 1:19 apply: "So then, my beloved brethren, let every man be swift to hear, slow to speak, slow to wrath." We need to be quick to hear God and slow to tell others what He has told us, so we will not be tempted to be angry with them when they do not catch our vision!

When I close my eyes to all the distractions and listen to God, it is then that I can hear that still, small voice telling me exactly what step to take next. It is true that without a vision the people perish. That is why the vision needs to be conceived in you first. Then it has to be walked out by faith, step by step.

This reminds me of the first time I learned I was pregnant. My husband, Bill, and I were considered "infertile" and had been trying to conceive for almost four years. That morning when I anxiously got up at 5:00 a.m. to take the pregnancy test and saw the first faint, positive sign, I hollered with glee, "Biiiill!! I'm pregnant!!" Needless to say, we were joyful! It wasn't long after that that the news was "noised abroad," and all our family and friends who were praying diligently for me to get pregnant were also joyful. I soon found out, however, that I had to walk the pregnancy out by faith, step by step!

Yes, there were trials along the way. A week or two after I found out I was pregnant, I was put on bed rest and given extra doses of progesterone in hopes that I would not miscarry. Not too long after that trial passed, nausea set in and I had to walk through morning sickness—or should I say all-day sickness? During this time, I remember thinking back on everything I had gone through to get pregnant and also having such joy looking forward to the day when the baby would be born and in my arms. I remember saying, "I want this baby so much, I will endure what I must to get it!" But for the joy set before me, I did endure! I still had to walk through other obstacles of pregnancy: having to watch carefully how much weight I gained, major swelling especially in my feet, the uncomfortable feeling at the end of the pregnancy (when the baby was so big she seemed to move in on the space that belongs to my organs!), and finally a very long and hard delivery. But in the end, it was worth it all!

Many of us are pregnant with the passions God has placed in us to one day accomplish for His glory. We must walk through each stage of pregnancy by faith, step by step. How does faith come? By hearing. And sometimes we have to close our eyes, knowing the big assignment is out there but not letting it distract us from hearing God's direction for each of the little steps that we must take to get there.

It is a biblical promise that if you are faithful in the small things, He will make you ruler over the larger things. Each time you take a step of faith and tell someone about Jesus, your faith will grow. I have found that there is no greater high than the high that comes after I have had the awesome privilege of sharing Christ with someone who does not know Him. Whether it is witnessing to someone, serving someone in love, spending time with God—whatever it is that the Holy Spirit is prompting us to do—as we walk those things out, we will be ready for bigger assignments. As we do, let us always remember that God gets all the glory!

"If anyone speaks, he should do it as one speaking the very words of God. If anyone serves, he should do it with the strength God provides, so that in all things God may be praised through Jesus Christ. To him be the glory and the power for ever and ever. Amen." 1 Peter 4:11 (NIV)

Going Deeper

Spiritually Pregnant
Read Luke 1:26-38.
Verse 27 - What indicates her purity?

Verse 28 – What did the angel call her?

Favor is a by-product of purity! Hearing God's Word and doing it leads to purity.
Verse 38 – What did Mary say?

When she said that, Jesus was conceived in her womb. When we read something in the Bible that stirs us, we need to be like Mary and say, "Let it be to me according to Your Word!" When we do, we become spiritually pregnant with the seed of the Word of God!

Don't Lose Sight of the Small Things!
Read Mark 10:13-16.
 Jesus and His disciples were going from place to place ministering to people when children were brought to Him for Him to touch and bless. The disciples probably thought the children were interfering with Jesus' important ministry schedule, but Jesus showed them that stopping to minister to the children *was* His important ministry opportunity.

In verse 15, what did Jesus say?

What characteristics of children do you think we need to have in order to inherit the Kingdom of God?

 Sometimes we do not want to do things that we do not consider "spiritual." However, when we are faithful with our everyday duties of this life, God will trust us with assignments for His Kingdom.

Read Luke 16:10-11. What do you sometimes consider unspiritual that God may be asking you to do?

If you start your day with a prayer that everything you do will be pleasing to Him, then everything you do that day will be "spiritual" because it is for Him!

Write out Matthew 25:21.

Prayer

Dear Lord, I want my whole life to be pleasing to You. Thank You for the passions and visions You are stirring in me. Help me not to miss out on the smaller ways in which I can serve You each day and help me to keep the "bigger vision" in perspective. I do not want the vision You have given me to distract me from hearing Your direction for each of the little steps that I must take to get there. Please help me to enjoy these assignments along the way. I choose to trust You in each step with simple, child-like faith. I praise You, for in You I am secure!

The Sense of Hearing

Day 5

Faith: Turning It On

T here are two aspects of faith—the person who has faith, and the person or object in which the person has placed his faith. We exercise faith every day. We have faith to believe that when we turn on a light switch—even though we do not actually see electricity or even understand how it works—the bulb will indeed light up. If we are not aware that the light bulb is burned out, we still exercise faith when we turn on the switch, but the bulb will not light up. The problem then lies not in the person who had the faith, but in the object in which the person has placed his faith. On the other hand, if the light bulb is not burned out and the source of electricity is available for the light bulb, it will still not light up if we do not exercise our faith and turn the switch on.

As Christians, we have faith in God. Unlike a light bulb, God will never let us down! There might be times when we think He has let us down, but when all is said and done and we have all the pieces to the puzzle, we will start to see why things happened the way they did. Sometimes we find out that when we thought God had forgotten about us, He was really protecting us.

"Now faith is the substance of things hoped for, the evidence of things not seen." Hebrews 11:1

The focus of this verse is not so much on the one with faith as it is on the One in whom faith lies. The Greek word for *substance* is *hupostasis.[1]* It comes from two words: *hupo[2]*– under, or place beneath, and *histemi*[3]– to stand; abide, continue, establish, hold up. In other words, God is our sure foundation Who holds us up and allows us to stand! The reason God is a sure foundation is that He is faithful! (See 1 Corinthians 1:9.) Since God is so faithful, our hope is also sure. When we hope in the Lord, we are not crossing our fingers, but we are anticipating with confidence, looking forward to what He is going to do in our lives. It is then that we begin to see with our spiritual eyes the evidence of our faith that is more sure than that which our physical eyes can see or our physical hands can touch.

"But without faith it is impossible to please Him, for he who comes to God must believe that He is, and that He is a rewarder of those who diligently seek Him." Hebrews 11:6

Even though God is faithful, we have to place our faith in Him, or faith will not be complete in us. If we do not exercise our faith in the spiritual — like we do in the natural when we turn on the light switch — we are not pleasing God. Faith is not only believing that God exists, but also believing that He is there to reach out to us. What good is praying if we do not believe He will answer our prayer? Faith that brings salvation has to have these two aspects of belief. Just knowing He is there, but not relying on Him to meet our needs is not faith. The Bible says that even the demons believe: "You believe that there is one God. Good! Even the demons believe that—and shudder" (James 2:19 NIV).

The demons do not just believe God exists; they *know* He does. One time Jesus approached a man who was demon-possessed; Jesus did not introduce Himself, but the man proclaimed who He was: "And he cried out with a loud voice and said, "What have I to do with You, Jesus, Son of the Most High God? I implore You by God that You do not torment me" (Mark 5:7).

There are many people in America—even in the church—who believe God exists, but they do not trust in Him to guide and direct their lives. Because they have not diligently sought Him, they have not experienced His rewards for living a godly life. He is pleased when we put our confidence in Him, and we are blessed beyond measure as He rewards us! As this happens we become part of the "evidence of things not seen." We will be like the trees when the wind blows. Though the wind itself cannot be seen, the limbs swaying back and forth are the evidence that the wind is blowing. Our lives should show the evidence of God's love in our words and actions. As Paul wrote in Galatians: "The only thing that counts is faith expressing itself through love" (Galatians 5:6b NIV). One by one, the people who observe the evidence in our lives will be drawn to God, and they too will experience the rewards of those who earnestly seek Him!

Going Deeper

How is faith developed?

According to John 6:44, before anyone can have faith, what has to happen?

Read Romans 10:14-17 and write in your own words the things that need to happen for faith to be developed in someone.

Compare Hebrews 4:2 and 1 Thessalonians 2:13. Some hear the Gospel, and it does not make a difference in their lives, while others hear it and it works effectively in them. What makes the difference?

As was mentioned before in this study, before we share the Gospel with people, we need to pray for the veil the enemy has over their eyes to be taken away and for the Holy Spirit to till the soil of their hearts.

Faith can grow! Read 2 Thessalonians 1:3 and write what also happens as our faith grows.

Abundant Life Through Faith

Part of faith is believing that God will reward us as we diligently seek Him. Read the following verses and write what we can have through faith according to each scripture passage:

Matthew 17:20 -

Matthew 21:22 -

Acts 3:16 -

Acts 11:15-17; Galatians 3:14 -

(For further study on the Promise of the Holy Spirit go to Luke 24:49, Acts 1:4-8, and the whole chapter of Acts 2.)

Romans 4:3 -

Romans 5:1, Galatians 3:24 -
(Note: "Justification" is "Just-as-if-I-had-never-sinned!")

Ephesians 3:12 -

Ephesians 3:17 -

Ephesians 6:16 -

James 5:14-16 -

1 Peter 1:5 -

1 John 5:4,5 -

The Opposite of Faith

Doubt and unbelief are the opposites of faith. What does James 1:6 say about one who doubts?

Write out the last sentence of Romans 14:23

The Testing of our Faith
In 1 Peter 1:6-7, what does Peter say is the reason we have trials?

According to James 1:3, what does the testing of our faith develop?

The Ultimate Revelation of our Faith
Part of the substance of things hoped for will be our glorious inheritance in Heaven! Read and meditate on 1 John 3:1-3: "Behold what manner of love the Father has bestowed on us, that we should be called children of God! Therefore the world does not know us, because it did not know Him. [2] Beloved, now we are children of God; and it has not yet been revealed what we shall be, but we know that when He is revealed, we shall be like Him, for we shall see Him as He is. [3] And everyone who has this hope in Him purifies himself, just as He is pure."

Prayer

Today, you need to compose the prayer as your response to what you studied. Please take time to write out your prayer. As you do, you will be amazed at how God will minister through you as you write. Also, you will be ministered to each time you go back and read it.

The Sense of Smell

"The fig tree puts forth her green figs, and the vines with the tender grapes give a good smell. Rise up, my love, my fair one, and come away!" Song of Solomon 2:13

Day 1

Smell: Making Sense of Scents

The sense of smell, also known as the olfactory system, is not emphasized as much as the other five senses. It seems to be the least understood of all the senses. However, after taking time to study how the sense of smell works, we will realize that it has more to do with how we function within our surroundings than we might have thought.

The organ with which we experience our sense of smell, the nose, is also used for breathing. The area in the nose used to process smells, the olfactory membrane, takes up only about five percent of the nasal cavity. There are actually two of these postage-stamp-size membranes—one for each side of the nose.

For us to be able to smell, the object being smelled must release molecules that are taken into our nose when we inhale. Everything we are able to smell gives off a scent with the release of tiny molecules—whether it is roses in a garden, bread baking in an oven, or sweaty tennis shoes in a locker. If something does not release these tiny molecules, it cannot be smelled. For instance, steel is odorless, because it is a non-volatile solid, and nothing evaporates from it.

The nasal cavity is lined with a mucous membrane. The olfactory membranes are protected with a thin coating of mucous. When the molecules are inhaled into the nose, the chemicals from the molecules are dissolved in the mucous before entering the olfactory membranes. When too much mucous is produced, for instance when we have a cold or allergies, the olfactory membrane is blocked, and we do not smell.

The olfactory membranes contain millions of nerve cells called olfactory receptor cells. At the end of the receptor cells are tiny hairs, or cilia, that collect the smell stimuli so that they may be sent to the brain. The longer one stays in an environment of a particular smell, he will begin to notice that the smell gets weaker—as if he is getting used to it. This happens because the receptors immediately gather the information from the stimuli and then cease to respond to it. Each receptor cell is connected to a part of the brain called the olfactory bulb by a singe cell, called a primary olfactory neuron. Because of this, the sense of smell is the most directly brain-linked sense. The other senses also send messages to the brain, but they must travel farther. The stimuli from the scents are then carried to the part of the brain that also processes memory and emotion. For this reason, smells are more closely related to memory than any other sense.

Studies have shown that people remember smells more easily and for longer periods of time than stimuli from other senses. In one study, people who were tested recalled up to sixty-five percent of smells a year after they first smelled them. The same people recalled only fifty percent of photographs after only four months of first seeing them.[1]

Odors also trigger emotions. The smell of chocolate chip cookies baking in the oven might remind someone of his grandmother. With the memory comes the same feeling of security and love he experienced in his grandmother's kitchen as a child. The smell of a certain perfume might remind someone of a friend or relative who wears the same perfume. The emotions triggered would depend on how that person feels about the person who wears that perfume.

The market place is booming these days with air fresheners, scented candles, colognes, and many other products that please our sense of smell. There are even certain scents used in oils, lotions and body sprays that are known to have therapeutic value. For instance, it is claimed that citrus scents help energize us while lavender scents are supposed to relax us and help us go to sleep. It is quite amazing that a fragrance that comes to us through our sense of smell can actually help to bring energy to a tired person or relaxation to someone who is stressed.

Another advantage of using our olfactory system is to keep us safe from harm. The smell of spoiled meat lets us know that we need to throw it out, rather than cook it and risk getting sick. Though natural gas is odorless, the gas companies have added an odor to it so that in the event of a potentially fatal gas leak, we can be warned to leave the premises and get the leak fixed.

As with the other four senses, God has blessed us with the sense of smell for us to enjoy life and to be kept safe from harm. We must not take this intricately designed system for granted! We are blessed when we smell the pot roast simmering for dinner, and we are definitely blessed when the smell of smoke prompts us to get our family out of a burning house. Whether it is for pleasure or safety, we need to remember to thank God for creating us with the ability to smell.

Going Deeper

Memory

As we have learned, the sense of smell is more closely related to memory than any of the other senses. Certain fragrances or odors trigger us to recall memories and often times experience the same feelings we had when the remembered event actually happened. Many of the memories are pleasant and include recollections of someone with whom we have enjoyed spending time. When that happens we need to stop and thank God.

What does Philippians 1:3 say?

Sometimes, the memories are not so pleasant. When a negative memory is triggered, we need to pray to God and ask Him to show us why we felt the way we did. It might be because our perception of the memory is marred by a lie of the enemy. (For example, someone may remember the day her parents divorced and believe the lie from the enemy that it was her fault that her parents divorced.) If that is the case, God will reveal the lie and give us His truth if we ask Him. He may speak to us with that still, small voice and bring us a comforting thought. He may simply give us a sense of peace that allows us to let go of the wrong perception. As was already mentioned in this study, many times the Holy Spirit will bring to mind a scripture that will answer the lies of Satan. Read the scriptures below and answer the questions.

1 John 4:18 – What casts out fear?
Who loves you perfectly?

Hebrews 13:5 – What did God say that will remind you that you do not have to feel lonely or abandoned?

Philippians 4:6-7 – When we are anxious, what should we do?

What will happen if we do that?

Read, underline, and memorize 1 John 1:9 and Romans 8:1 so that you can quote them next time Satan tries to condemn you about a past sin:

Being Desensitized to the Scent

If we are in a room with an offensive odor, we will be desensitized to that odor after a while and not notice the smell. In the same way, we as Christians can be desensitized to the evil in the world if we are not careful. As we approach the day when Christ returns, the Bible warns us that evil will increase. The problem is that some in the church are turning their heads to the evil, not calling sin what it is because they do not want to offend anyone. Not only that, some are starting to embrace those things and even practice them. When that happens, the church will not be the "salt of the earth" (Matthew 5:13).

Read the following verses that will remind us to not be desensitized to the world and answer the questions.

Romans 12:2 – What are we not supposed to be conformed to?

Instead we are to be transformed by _____.

If that happens, what will we be able to do?

Ephesians 5:8-14 – According to verse 11, what are we to not have fellowship with?

What are we supposed to do instead?

1 John 2:15-17 – What are we not supposed to love?
What is passing away?
What will not pass away?

Prayer

Lord, I thank You for the amazing sense of smell. Thank You that with it I have pleasure and am warned of danger. Help me to not take it for granted. I pray also for my mind. I need to be transformed by the renewing of my mind. I need your perspective on my memories. I also need Your perspective on this world and the people around me. Help me to remember that I am in the world, but I am not of it. I do not want to be influenced by those people in the world who do not know You, but instead I want to be salt to them and influence them for Your kingdom.

The Sense of Smell

Day 2

Misuse Hinders Our Discernment

I n his book, *Fresh Wind, Fresh Fire,* Jim Cymbala, pastor of the Brooklyn Tabernacle church in New York, told of a time at the end of a service when he invited everyone who wanted to accept Christ into his or her life to come down to the altar. A homeless man came down who was very dirty, with grime caked on his body and matted in his hair. Jim said that the man had an odor of sweat and urine so nauseating that Jim would turn his head to inhale and look toward the man as he breathed out. God convicted Jim and let him know how much He loved this homeless man. Jim repented to the Lord. Just then, the man fell on Jim's chest and embraced him. Jim said that at that point, the offensive smell actually began to be pleasant as he led the man to the Lord. Jim recalls in his book, "The Lord seemed to say to me in that instant, *Jim, if you and your wife have any value to me, if you have any purpose in my work—it has to do with this odor. This is the smell of the world I died for.*"[1] Thank God, the homeless man surrendered his life to Christ.

How many people who had come into this man's life could have helped him but turned away because of his offensive odor? What would have happened if Jim Cymbala had said, "Well, we'll just let God deal with that man; I can't even get close to him, or I'll get sick"? In that case, the sense of smell would be a hindrance to discernment of the man's desperate need for God. Or maybe the man's need would be obvious, but the desire for self-comfort would be stronger than the desire to rescue him. The result? Lack of discernment that resulted in a squandered opportunity to win his soul, perhaps the last chance to do so in that man's life. How sad! Praise God that did not happen in this case, but how many times in street ministry (or lack of street ministry due to people's desire for self-comfort) has that happened?

Most scents we just pick up without even trying to smell them. We smell automatically when we breathe, and we have to breathe to live. But sometimes what we breathe in can be harmful, even fatal. Second-hand smoke from cigarettes (also known as environmental tobacco smoke or ETS) is one of those things that we sometimes cannot help but inhale, and it is deadly. According to a 1993 report by the United States Environmental Protection Agency, exposure to ETS causes approximately 3,000 lung cancer deaths to nonsmokers in the United States each year. Second-hand smoke also increases the risk of asthma and other respiratory infections such as bronchitis and pneumonia. Children are especially vulnerable with between 150,000 and 300,000 of these cases in babies up to 18 months each year. ETS had also led to chronic middle ear infections in some children.[2] Children with one or both parents who smoke will have their chances doubled of developing severe upper respiratory problems, ear infections, and allergies. And while smoking parents think they are protecting their children by going outside to smoke, when they come back in and hug their children, they still are putting them at risk, because even cigarette-smoke residue in clothing negatively affects health. Besides that, by smoking, they are setting a bad example before their children to smoke. I venture to say that if you ask a smoker if his parents smoked when he was a child, most would say yes. Whether a smoker realizes this is happening or not, he is allowing the desire for a little pleasure from smoking to over rule the discernment that he is causing harm to others—especially his children.

Studies on the effects of smoking, both to the smoker and the non-smoker, all agree that the habit leads to death. There is no good thing that comes from it. Yes, there may be pleasure or a sense of relaxation for the smoker, but those pleasures lead to destruction. Can a person smoke and be a Christian? Yes. However, smoking is not God's best for anyone. Each of our bodies is the temple of the Holy Spirit. God deserves a temple that is healthy! Besides that, a Christian witness is greatly hindered when others observe a smoker lighting up. Whoever reads this either knows a smoker or is a smoker. We need to pray that the strongholds of addiction in the lives of smokers will be destroyed and that whatever lie the enemy has sold them that would keep them bound to nicotine would be revealed and healed.

While inhaling smoke is not always intentional, the number of young people who do inhale drugs in order to get a high is a serious problem. Many of them inhale chemicals from household cleaning solutions and other things that are readily available in any home. This occurs at a higher rate in children than in older teens and adults, and many parents do not have a clue that their child is addicted. The age group most involved with using inhalants is middle-school-age children. Sniffing chemicals found in cleaning solutions, spray paint, magic markers, correction fluid, cooking oil sprays, canned whipped cream, and other items, often leads the child to eventually use stronger illegal drugs as inhalants. What is sad is that inhaling drugs for a temporary high or euphoric sensation damages brain cells that are irreplaceable. Other health problems caused by sniffing drugs include heart problems and diminished cognitive abilities, as well as damage to the optic nerve, kidneys, liver and bones, and death due to suffocation.[3] Again, the temporary high ends up winning the battle over any discernment in the child that these things are deadly. Tragically, the result is fatal.

We need to be aware that the enemy wants to come in any gate he can to destroy and to keep us from being effective for God's kingdom. Our noses are no exception. Satan also uses our sense of smell so that we will offend others when we show our disapproval of their odor. For instance, if someone is stirred of the Holy Spirit to minister in a nursing home but then walks in a room and turns his head in disgust from an offensive odor, how can he truly show the love of Christ to the person in need? God will help us to overcome these situations if we ask Him. The closer we get to God, the more He will give us discernment to turn away from harmful odors, yet endure the stench of this world so that we may rescue the perishing.

Going Deeper

Don't Let Offensive Odors Hinder You!

As Christians, we need to be ready in our churches to welcome the people society considers outcasts. We are supposed to be going out to the highways and byways and compelling people to come in (Luke 14:23). When we do that, the people in the church need to be ready to receive people off the streets who may not be dressed nicely or even bathed.

Read James 2:1-13 and answer the following questions:
Verse 1 – We are warned not to _____.

Verses 2-4 – How do we show partiality in the way we treat different people?

Verse 5 – What has God chosen the poor of this world to be?

Verses 6 and 7 remind us that the rich, whom we have a tendency to show partiality toward, sometimes oppress us. How do they oppress us?

Verse 8 – What is the "royal law" this verse talks about?

Verse 9 – What action does this verse call showing partiality?

Verse 10 – If you do that, what part of the law are you guilty of?

Verse 13 – What triumphs over judgment that we need to show others?

We need to remember that Jesus showed no favoritism. In biblical times, lepers were thought of as unclean. They were outcasts, and no one approached them. I am sure that with the open sores of lepers also came a disgusting odor. Yet Jesus showed mercy to them by going right to them, touching them and healing them. (See one example of this in Matthew 8:1-3.) We cannot confess what our nose is telling us when we are in a situation like this. When we do, we speak death instead of life to the person (Proverbs 18:21).

Be a Godly Example

Children who grow up in families where one or both parents smoke are more likely to start smoking as teenagers, or even as preteens. This is just one example of how children will start imitating parents' behavior without the parents even realizing the impact they have on their children. Other examples include anger, gossiping, slander, over-eating, drinking, and other compulsive behaviors. Paul admonished Timothy to be an example of godly living as a young person. How much more do children look to their parents as examples of how to live? Every one of us influences the people around us whether we are parents or not.

Read 1 Timothy 4:12 and write down what we are to be examples in.

Knowing that we are examples for others around us should remind us to think of others in our actions, and not just ourselves. Think about this as you read Philippians 2:3-4.

Prayer

Father, I pray for protection of my "nose gate." I pray for protection over my loved ones and myself from anything that would harm us through our sense of smell. I also pray for discernment for myself and for my loved ones to turn away from harmful odors. Thank You for giving me strength and self-control to endure the stench of this world, so that I might help to rescue the perishing. I want to show Your mercy to those around me so that they will see Your love and be drawn to You. I choose to seek You for direction to do that which is pleasing to You and to let You live through me as an example to those You place in my life. In Jesus Name, Amen!

The Sense of Smell

Day 3

We Are an Aroma

I recently heard a story about two men who partnered together selling produce at a busy farmer's market. One man sold herbs; the other man sold vegetables. The one who sold herbs would kick the basil basket to release the aroma, and people would come from a block away to find out where the delicious smell originated. Not only would the sales of his herbs increase when he kicked the basil, but his friend also benefited by selling more vegetables. The people all around then had a newfound awareness of the produce.

My prayer is that my life would emit an aroma that would cause an awareness of God in the people around me. Paul wrote about us being an aroma in 2 Corinthians 2:14-16a: "Now thanks be to God who always leads us in triumph in Christ, and through us diffuses the fragrance of His knowledge in every place. For we are to God the fragrance of Christ among those who are being saved and among those who are perishing. To the one we are the aroma of death leading to death, and to the other the aroma of life leading to life." At the time Paul wrote this, the Roman custom after a war was to have a triumphant parade led by the captain of the winning army. Behind the chariot of the victorious army captain followed the "winnings"—including the captain of the losing army stripped of all his honors with his army and all of their livestock and other goods. I can imagine the line of former POWs (prisoners of war) now released also following behind, but instead of being chained, they are dancing in the streets!

At these parades, it was also the custom to burn incense to the gods in thanksgiving. However, in Christ's parade, we are the incense to the only true God who deserves all the thanks and praise! We must remember that this "incense" is toward God, not to the people. They do, however, notice it and smell it as well. When they do, their attention is drawn to God, not to us. Some smell the aroma and are led to abundant life in Christ as the Holy Spirit draws them. Others, influenced by the enemy of their soul, smell it and are repulsed by anyone's attempt to point to their need for a savior.

It does not matter what we go through, God causes us to triumph! We have to remember that it is not about us. If we look at the verses before this verse in 1 Corinthians 1 and 2, we realize by Paul's words that he had just gone through some very trying times. He reminds us that trials are allowed by God to bring about purposes that far exceed the pain of the current situation that seems to be destroying us. He also encouraged those to whom he wrote to not take offense at whoever caused his pain, but to forgive them "lest Satan should take advantage of us; for we are not ignorant of his devices" (1 Corinthians 2:11).

It is when we go through trials that we have the opportunity to be that fragrance to God through Christ. People in the church and outside the church watch how we handle adversity. We suffer for many reasons. Sometimes we are grieved because of our own sinful mistakes, and we have to suffer the consequences. But even then, God can turn it around for us and cause good to come from it for eternal value if we let Him. Other times, our suffering has absolutely nothing to do with our sin. As was mentioned on Day 4 of "Sight," it is imperative that we keep the right focus. Our spirits need to say to God, "Lord, I am willing to suffer for You!" When we do, it will be as Paul encouraged in the opening chapter of 1 Corinthians: "For as the sufferings of Christ abound in us, so our consolation also abounds through Christ." As sure as the sufferings are in our lives, so also is the promise that we will follow Christ in a triumphant parade and be vessels to "diffuse the fragrance of His knowledge in every place"—all because of what Christ did for us. We do not have to work at winning the victory. We just have to enter into the triumph He has already won for us!

In the Old Testament, animals were killed as a sacrifice for people's sins. The smell of burning flesh is rancid! Yet it was a sweet-smelling savor to the Lord because of man's obedience to His commands. "And you shall burn the whole ram on the altar. It is a burnt offering to the Lord; it is a sweet aroma, an offering made by fire to the Lord" Exodus 29:18.

If the burning sacrifices of the Old Testament were pleasing to God, how much more was Christ's sacrifice pleasing to God? The Old Testament sacrifices did meet the requirement that blood must be shed for the remission of sins (Hebrews 9:22). However, the sacrifices were not perfect, so the high priest had to offer them yearly. The good news is that Jesus came to be the High Priest *and* the sacrificial lamb! This points to why it was important that He be fully human (the priest is a man who represents the people to God) and fully God (only God could be perfect enough for the sacrifice to be offered once for all and not have to be done yearly).

"But Christ came as High Priest of the good things to come, with the greater and more perfect tabernacle not made with hands, that is, not of this creation. Not with the blood of goats and calves, but with His own blood He entered the Most Holy Place once for all, having obtained eternal redemption. For if the blood of bulls and goats and the ashes of a heifer, sprinkling the unclean, sanctifies for the purifying of the flesh, how much more shall the blood of Christ, who through the eternal Spirit offered Himself without spot to God, cleanse your conscience from dead works to serve the living God?" Hebrews 9:11-14

As Christians, we are encouraged to enter into what Christ did for us at the cross and "die" to our fleshly desires: "I have been crucified with Christ; it is no longer I who live, but Christ lives in me; and the life which I now live in the flesh I live by faith in the Son of God, who loved me and gave Himself for me" (Galatians 2:20).

When we let our desires be "crucified" and exchanged for God's desires, then we are a sweet-smelling savor to God. This also means that we will not bow down to the natural tendencies that our minds dwell on. Often times, it is human nature to see the negative in a situation first. We may be served great food at a restaurant, but if the service is not as fast as we would like, our tendency might be to focus on the lack of service instead of the great food. When that happens, we end up not even enjoying our food. Some people take it to the next step and let everyone around know about their dissatisfaction. We need to pray to God to help us to focus on the good in every situation. As spouses, parents, teachers and friends, are we too busy pointing out people's weaknesses, or do we "consider one another in order to stir up love and good works" (Hebrews 10:24)? Continued nagging does not stir up love and good works! And it does not allow us to be a sweet-smelling aroma of Christ's love to those around us.

The only way we will be such an aroma to God and those around us is by love. As 2 Corinthians 5:14-17 says, "For the love of Christ compels us, because we judge thus: that if One died for all, then all died; and He died for all, that those who live should live no longer for themselves, but for Him who died for them and rose again. Therefore, from now on, we regard no one according to the flesh. Even though we have known Christ according to the flesh, yet now we know Him thus no longer. Therefore, if anyone is in Christ, he is a new creation; old things have passed away; behold, all things have become new."

I recently heard it taught that Paul was not talking about Christ's love for us, but rather our love for Christ that compels us. I can see where it is really both. It is because of His love in the first place that He offered Himself for us so that we could enter into His sacrifice and be crucified with Him. However, if we do not respond back with a love for Christ, there is no way we will live for Him and go through all the suffering that we sometimes have to go through as Christians. Another version of the Bible says that the love of Christ "constrains" us. Yet another translation uses the word "controls." Christ does not control us against our will. His desire is that the fruit of the Spirit of self-control be developed in us. When we truly love Christ, that love will be the reason we put controls on our fleshly desires and do what we know pleases God through the power of the

Holy Spirit. It is then that we follow Christ's example and walk in true love.

"And walk in love, as Christ also has loved us and given Himself for us, an offering and a sacrifice to God for a sweet-smelling aroma." Ephesians 5:2

Going Deeper

Going Through the Fire
The scent of incense is stronger when it is burned. If we want to be an aroma that will draw people to God, we must be willing to go through the fire.

Read Isaiah 43:1-2. What happens to those who are redeemed by God when they have to go through the fire?

If we remember this promise when we are going through great trials, it will be easier to endure.

Read and underline 2 Corinthians 1:3-4.

Read 2 Corinthians 1:8-11 and answer the following questions:

Verse 8 – Write the words that tell us how much despair Paul was in.

Notice that he does not give details about what happened to cause this. We do not have to know all the details about why someone is suffering to be able to hold them up in prayer. (Neither do we need to tell people all the details about what we are going through.)
Verse 9 – What reason does Paul give that they had to be in this desperate state?

Verse 10 – This is a reminder (and a focus check!) of God's deliverance in the past, present and future. That is why we can trust Him!
Verse 11 – How did the people help Paul?

Being a Sacrifice to the Lord

Just as the Old Testament sacrifices were pleasing to the Lord, He is also pleased when we offer ourselves to Him.

"I beseech you therefore, brethren, by the mercies of God, that you present your bodies a living sacrifice, holy, acceptable to God, which is your reasonable service. [2] And do not be conformed to this world, but be transformed by the renewing of your mind, that you may prove what is that good and acceptable and perfect will of God." Romans 12:1-2

Verse 1 - In what ways do you think you can *"present your bodies a living sacrifice"* to the Lord?

(In light of the title of this book, *Loving God With All Five Senses,* one way is to not over-indulge in the desires of the senses, or gratification of the flesh. The act of offering our desires in exchange for God's desires for us may seem difficult at first, but in the end it brings total freedom!)

Verse 2 – What are some patterns or tendencies of the world that we should not be conformed to?

Read and underline Philippians 4:8. Meditate on what the verse says about what we are to allow our minds to dwell on.

Our Prayers: An Incense to God

Prayer is such a vital part of our walk with God. Read the following scriptures that address incense representing the prayers of the saints:

Psalm 141:2   Revelation 5:8   Revelation 8:3-4

In the Old Testament, incense was burned often unto the Lord. The burning of incense was especially important in the Tabernacle.

The Tabernacle

After the children of Israel escaped from Egypt, God gave Moses specific instructions to set up the Tabernacle as a place for the people to meet with God. This Tabernacle was set up in a tent surrounded by a courtyard. The layout of the Tabernacle symbolizes how we can approach God:

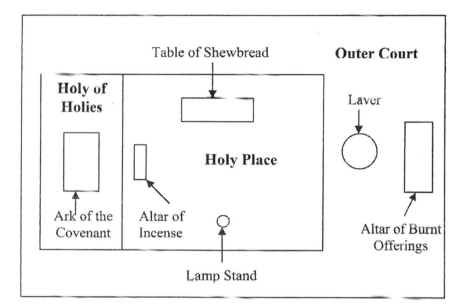

- **The Brazen Altar** was set up inside the entrance of the courtyard for sacrifices to be made for the sins of the people. *The first step to approach God is to accept Christ's sacrifice for one's sins.*

- **The Brass Laver** was the next item on the way to the tabernacle. It was where the priests washed to prepare themselves to enter the Holy Place. *Even after we accept Christ's sacrifice and are saved, we need to "wash" daily by confessing our sins and reading His Word. This also symbolizes the importance of water baptism.*

- Next was the Tabernacle that had a veil dividing the Holy Place and the Holy of Holies. As the priest entered the Holy

Place, there was **the Lampstand** fueled by oil on the left (south) and **the Table of Shewbread** on the right (north). The priests tended to the Lampstand by trimming the wicks and adding oil each morning and evening so that the flame would never go out. The Table of Shewbread had 12 loaves of unleavened bread, one representing each tribe of Israel, that the priests would eat. *Since the Holy Spirit guides us into all truth, and Jesus (the Word and the Bread of Life) is truth, this symbolizes the Holy Spirit illuminating the Word of God as we read it.*

- Just before the veil to the Holy of Holies was **the Altar of Incense**. This was to burn continually with not just any spices, but those laid out by God to be used specifically for the Tabernacle. *This represents our prayers of praise, worship and requests according to His will that allow us to enter into the Most Holy of Holies with boldness because of what Christ did for us! It reminds us to always have an attitude of prayer and praise so that we can "pray without ceasing." It also reminds us to not just pray in any way—for example praying for our own desires without seeking what He desires—but to pray according to His will.*

- Only the high priest could go past the veil into the Holy of Holies where the **Ark of the Covenant** and God's manifest presence were. Later, the Temple was set up the same way. The good news is that when Jesus breathed His last breath on the cross, the veil that separated the Holy Place from the Holy of Holies in the Temple was ripped apart from the top to the bottom. (See Mark 15:37-39 and Hebrews 10:19-20.) *Now anyone, not just the high priest, can go where His manifest presence is at any time! We are now the temple where the Great High Priest resides. As soon as we burn the incense with a whispered prayer, we are there!*

Prayer

Lord, I thank You that Your fullness dwells in me! Please take away the clutter in my life that would keep me from recognizing that. Thank You that I am the temple of the Holy Spirit. I pray that my life would be one that You can use to diffuse the fragrance of Your knowledge everywhere I go. When I go through the fire of testing, help me to remember that as sure as the sufferings will come, so the consolation will come through You (2 Corinthians 1:5). I pray that the way I handle the trials by leaning on You will be an aroma that leads those around me to You. Thank You that I can come boldly into the Holy of Holies, and that You are there the minute I need You—which is every minute! I love You, Lord!

The Sense of Smell

Day 4

Spiritual Breathing

B efore we delve deeper into the subject of discernment, I would like to touch on the other job of our nose—breathing. As we learned on Day 1 of "Smell," smelling takes place in only five percent of the nasal cavity. The other ninety-five percent is used for breathing. God made our noses so that the hairs and the mucus would filter out any dust or foreign particles before the air we inhale reaches our lungs. In the back of the nasal cavity is the pharynx that is shared by the digestive system. The dust and particles either go down the pharynx and are swallowed into the stomach, where the digestive enzymes destroy them, or they are sneezed out or blown out when we blow our nose. Just in case anything gets past all that in our noses, there are also hair-like cilia within the bronchial tubes that constantly move upward to keep particles out of the lungs. Basically, God created us with an incredible filtering system to keep us safe from harmful germs or foreign particles that would clog our air passages or hinder our breathing.

Just as God has created a great filtering system in our natural bodies, His Word is a great filtering system for our spirits. The NIV Bible says in 2 Timothy 3:16 that the scripture is "God-breathed." It can be used to help filter things in our lives.

We need to remember that we humans were created differently than any other life form, because God breathed life into us. As was mentioned in "Going Deeper" of "Taste" Day 1, the Hebrew word for "breath" is "ruwach," which is also translated, "the Spirit of God." It was God who breathed into us, and it is God who breathes into our spirits when we read the Bible! Jesus is the Word in flesh. The Holy Spirit reveals Jesus to us in the written Word. As He does, He uses the awesome truths in His Word to help filter the things we allow to enter our spirits.

In "Going Deeper" of "Taste" Day 4, we looked closely at 2 Timothy 3:16-17. For our study on spiritual breathing, I would like to look at verse 16 again. The NKJV says: "All Scripture is given by inspiration of God, and is profitable for doctrine, for reproof, for correction, for instruction in righteousness." Study of the Bible is profitable for 4 things:

1. <u>Doctrine</u> – Doctrine lets us know what is right and wrong and is the first step to discernment.
2. <u>Reproof</u> – Reproof means "to express disapproval of." If we fail to heed to the doctrine we are taught, reproof reminds us to turn from sin.
3. <u>Correction</u> – To correct is the next step needed after one sins to help him get back on track.
4. <u>Instruction in Righteousness</u> – Continued instruction from the Word is preventative maintenance.

That is how the Bible works as a great filtering system that leads to discernment! We really cannot have discernment without the study of the Bible. When we allow God to use His Word in those four ways in our lives, we are allowing Him to breathe for us and give us inspiration!

Allowing the Lord to breathe into our spirits will bring a peace and calmness in the midst of any storm. In natural childbirth classes, the mother is taught breathing techniques that help bring extra oxygen needed to release physical tension and also help to get her mind focused to release emotional tension. When we go through trials, a good exercise is to take a deep breath (imagining we are breathing in Jesus) and blow out (imagining we are exhaling anxieties). When we do that, it is merely a reminder to seek God's perspective on our circumstances instead of dwelling frantically on the "what if" and "if only" thoughts that bring anxiety.

As the old saying goes, we need to "let go and let God." Many will say, "That is easier said than done. You don't know what I'm going through." That might be true, but many do not experience the peace of letting God take care of them, because they have not really asked Him to. The Bible says that we have not, because we ask not. It also says if we ask anything according to His will, He will hear and answer. We need to say a simple prayer to ask God to forgive us for trying to run our own lives and tell Him we want to let go and let Him take control. If we ask with faith, believing that He will guide and direct us, He will!

The problem most of us have is that we have a hard time letting go of the reigns. We want to run our own lives. Steve McVey talks about this in his book *Grace Walk*:

"As part of my pastoral responsibilities, I have visited many hospitals. On numerous occasions I have seen people on a respirator. I've watched people wake up on a breathing machine after open-heart surgery. Certain people have real trouble with those machines. It's the people who try who run into trouble. The respirator is built to do the breathing. The patient just needs to relax. But when a person panics and tries to breathe, alarms beep, and the patient is uncomfortable, because he is working against a machine that is designed to breathe for him."

He goes on to say,

"Living the Christian life is similar to breathing...God never intended for the Christian life to be a struggle. The Holy Spirit should flow from the life of the Christian as naturally as breathing. But many Christians are hyperventilating trying to do something for God."[1]

As we learn to surrender to God, we will then allow His Spirit to breathe through us and bring us abundant life. Only then can we enter into His rest and have fulfillment in our lives.

Going Deeper

As Natural as Breathing

Every human has a void in his life that can only be filled by having a relationship with God. He is not just "the man upstairs," but He is a personal God who wants to be there to guide our lives and give us peace, hope and love as only He can do. When we let Him take the reigns and guide our lives (even asking His guidance for the little things), it becomes a lifestyle that is as natural as breathing. When we get off track and go through with Satan's temptation for us to take back the reigns and make our own decisions without God, we get a spiritual respiratory infection! However, if we heed the written prescriptions in the Bible, we will get better and have that peace in the midst of whatever we go through as we allow God to take control again.

It is not "being religious" that brings the ease of spiritual breathing. When we go through all the motions of religion, trying to reach up to God through activities done by rote, it is like we are trying to breathe for the breathing machine that is supposed to breathe for us. God is reaching down to us. We simply need to acknowledge that and let Him!

Read Acts 17:22-28. The people Paul was addressing were very religious people with a desire to worship, but they did not even know God. Which verse of this scripture passage indicates that God desires a personal relationship with everyone?

God's Breath Brings Life or Destruction

What do the following scriptures say about the breath of God?

Psalm 33:6 -

Job 33:4 -

John 20:22 -

As we have seen, God's breath can bring life to us. Those who continue living to fulfill selfish desires will experience destruction from the breath of God instead of life.

What does Job 4:8-9 say about those who "plow iniquity?"

Look at what 2 Thessalonians 2:8 says will happen to the anti-Christ.

> "And then the lawless one will be revealed,
> whom the Lord will consume with
> the breath of His mouth and destroy with
> the brightness of His coming."

The Bible says that every knee will bow and every tongue will confess that Jesus is God. It is far better to bow to Him now, because we love Him and want a relationship with Him, than it will be to wait until we have to at the judgment. We will also be spared from being destroyed with His breath if we allow Him to breathe life into our spirits now.

God's Breath Brings Life to Dry Bones

Ezekiel 37:1-14 is a prophesy about the nation of Israel coming together by the Spirit of God. As I read it I also think of churches today that are dry and lifeless. As you read this passage, notice that even when the bones came together with sinews, flesh and skin, there was still no life in them until the breath of God came into them. Write a prayer that God will bring life to the dryness of your church, family and self through the power of His Holy Spirit.

Letting Go and Letting God

Read 1 Peter 5:6-7. Verse 6 tells us to humble ourselves, and God will exalt us in time. How does verse 7 tell us to do that?

Read Matthew 11:28-30. Take time to meditate on what Jesus is telling you and respond to him in prayer.

Prayer

Thank You, dear Lord, for being a personal God who longs to have a relationship with me! I want it to be as natural for me to allow You to guide and direct my life as it is to breathe. Thank You that Your Word is a filter for my spirit. I am grateful for each time You reveal the truths in Your Word, oh Holy Spirit. Help me to grow in You and learn how to truly let go of the reigns of my life and allow You to take control of my life. I thank you for Your peace that will guide my heart and mind as I surrender to You on a daily basis. Thank You that when I forget that and start being anxious, You are still as close as the mention of Your name. I choose to exhale anxieties and inhale Your Spirit! How awesome that the Creator of the universe is there for me at all times! My desire to worship is satisfied as I return Your love!

The Sense of Smell

Day 5

Discernment: What is Going On?

From the first day of a baby's life, he is taking in data about his new world by way of each of the five senses. The sense of smell is no exception. One reason an infant's cry calms when his mother picks him up is that he knows his mother's scent. When he smells (and thus discerns) that he is in his mother's arms and not someone else's, his anxieties vanish.

To have discernment means to be aware of what is around you. Infants start discerning from the moment they are born. So the first prerequisite to having discernment is to be born! The same thing goes for having spiritual discernment.

There is a very real spiritual realm that we cannot see with our natural eyes. The demonic hosts and the angelic hosts are involved in spiritual warfare all around us. Most people are not even aware of this reality. One reason could be because they have not yet been born of the Spirit. When they choose to trust in Jesus as their Lord and Savior, the Bible says that the Holy Spirit comes to dwell in them and their spirit is then born within them. Until then, they cannot discern the things of the Spirit. "These things we also speak, not in words which man's wisdom teaches but which the Holy Spirit teaches, comparing spiritual things with spiritual. But the natural man does not receive the things of the Spirit of God, for they are foolishness to him; nor can he know them, because they are spiritually discerned" 1 Corinthians 2:13-14.

As a child grows, he learns more and more about his surroundings through the things he is taught, and more concretely through the things he experiences; consequently his discernment also grows. However, just the passage of time does not guarantee that discernment has developed. Maturity is what brings deeper discernment, and physical growth does not necessarily indicate increasing maturity. In our society, a child must go to school, study what is taught, and apply it to his life in order to become mature. If a child never went to school, his maturity level would be limited. By going to school and mastering the skills needed in each grade, the child's capacity for more maturity grows until one day he matures into an adult. Then he is able to make his own decisions and take care of himself and a family.

There are many Christians sitting in the pews who do not have much discernment. Like the non-believer, they are not aware of the things going on in the spiritual realm all around them. The missing link is discipleship. Just like a child must go to school and study to develop the skills and discernment necessary to live a successful life, so a child of God needs to "study to show himself approved" (1 Timothy 2:15) so that he can make the right choices and receive the wisdom God desires to give him.

It is not God's will for us to remain infants in the faith (Hebrews 5:12-14). God desires for us to have an intimate, personal relationship with Him. When that spark for intimacy with God is lit deep within the spirit of a person, he will then want to do those things that please the Father (2 Corinthians 5:9). Not only will he have the desire to please God, but he will know what to do to please God and when to do it, because the more time he spends with God, the more he gets to know God. As he gets to know God, he will also learn how to be led by God. That is when discipleship becomes a joyous, exciting adventure instead of a dreaded obligation.

With discipleship comes discipline. Punishment carried out in the right way brings training. Parents who discipline in a godly manner do so for the child's protection or to teach the child a lesson—not as an outlet of anger for the parent. Chastisement is never meant to heap guilt or condemnation on the child, but rather a conviction to do what is right. "No discipline seems pleasant at the time, but painful. Later on, however, it produces a harvest of righteousness and peace for those who have been trained by it" Hebrews 12:11 (NIV).

As parents we need to check our motivation when we discipline our children. God, on the other hand, always has the right motivation when He chastises us. If we feel guilt or condemnation, it is not from God! (See Romans 8:1.) What God has in mind for us is righteousness and peace! When we go through trials, it will be easier to endure the pain if we remember that on the other side of the trial is a life of righteousness and peace! We need to seek God to find out what He is trying to teach us. Even if the trial is not brought about because of something we have done wrong, if we worry and fret in the midst of it, God will bring correction to us to get our focus back on Him, the problem solver, instead of the problem.

The goal of discipline is not just to teach a child the lesson of the moment, but more far-reaching than that, the objective is to have the child learn to discipline himself and allow the fruit of self-control to be developed in him. I have been known to tell my children to check their attitude, or I would have to help them adjust their attitude! Sometimes that warning is all they need to get back on the right track. Other times they do not change their attitude on their own, and they have to endure a time of punishment. As Christians, we need to have periodic attitude checks. If we are wise, we will examine ourselves and seek God to help us get back on track when He reveals to us problems in our attitudes. If we do not heed the gentle stirring of the Spirit to stop a particular thought pattern or action, we will have to endure a harder time of chastisement. "But if we judged ourselves, we would not come under judgment. When we are judged by the Lord, we are being disciplined so that we will not be condemned with the world" 1 Corinthians 11:31-32 (NIV).

Though we will go through times of testing and chastisement, we can also avoid some hard times by making right choices. When we can discern between good and evil ahead of time, then we are able to steer clear of a situation that would bring harm or temptation to us. I recently saw an interview on a news broadcast of a family who has trained their two dogs to warn them before their children have a diabetic seizure. The children each have a dog that stays with them everywhere they go. When their blood sugar is low, the dog detects the change in scent that accompanies the chemical change in the child's body. The dog then jumps on the child, barks, and licks his face to let him know he needs to take in sugar before a seizure occurs. One of the children, who previously had suffered multiple seizures weekly or even daily, reported that he has had only one seizure since owning the dog, and that was when the dog was at the veterinarian's office.

We have something better than a dog with us at all times to warn us of danger. We have the Holy Spirit, the omniscient God, dwelling within our spirits! We need to pay more attention to the prompting of the Holy Spirit and thus learn discernment from the One who discerns all. As that discernment develops within us and we heed the Spirit's prompting, we will make decisions that will either keep us from going through certain trials or help us keep the correct perspective while going through a trial.

Going Deeper

Growing into Maturity

The importance of developing an intimate relationship with God has been discussed throughout this book. When a person does become intimate with Christ, he will start maturing in Christ. Sometimes we get our focus off Christ and act out in immature ways. We all do it from time to time. I have learned that when I act out immaturely, it is more than likely a time when I am slack in my "alone time" with God. (Note: After spending quality time alone with God in praise, worship, prayer and Bible study, you can learn how to have "alone time" with God even when you are in a crowd!) Many Christians— including people who have been Christians for many years—seldom have the time the alone with God needed to develop maturity.

Read Hebrews 5:12-14 and answer the following questions:

Verse 12 – What did the author of Hebrews say to indicate that those to whom he wrote had been believers for a long time?

What do you think this verse is referring to when it says "milk" and "solid food?"

Verse 13 – What does this verse call those who partake only of "milk?"

Verse 14 in the NKJV says, "But solid food belongs to those who are of full age, that is, those who by reason of use have their senses exercised to discern both good and evil."

This verse points to the "senses" in the spiritual realm, for example when Jesus said, "He who has ears, let him hear," or when we are asked to "look unto Jesus." However, as we have already learned, the natural senses can also be used to hinder or promote spiritual maturity.

Discipline Brings Maturity and Discernment

The passages that we just read talk about "babes" partaking of "milk" instead of "solid food." Infants are not punished. As they grow, it is necessary for many reasons for them to start being disciplined from time to time. After someone gets saved and begins to grow in the Lord, he will begin to be disciplined. We need to learn to welcome the chastening of the Lord, for it means we are growing. It would be sad to remain as infants.

Read the following scripture passages, and tell what each one says about why we are disciplined:

Proverbs 3:11,12 -

John 15:2 -

1 Corinthians 11:32 -

2 Corinthians 12:7 -

Keep reading verses 8 and 9. Even though we are punished, what does God offer us?

Hebrews 12:10,11 -

Read the following passage from the New King James version of the Bible:

> "And this I pray, that your love may abound still more and more in knowledge and all discernment, [10] that you may approve the things that are excellent, that you may be sincere and without offense till the day of Christ, [11] being filled with the fruits of righteousness which are by Jesus Christ, to the glory and praise of God." Philippians 1:9-11

The desire of Paul's heart when he wrote this to the church of Philippi was that as they grew and developed discernment, they would also "be without offense." In other words, he did not want them to carry a grudge against anyone—no matter what anyone did to them or said about them. He also prayed that they would be filled with the fruits of righteousness. As we have already seen in Hebrews 12:11, this comes from discipline.

What is My Part in Developing Discernment?
Spiritual discernment is really godly wisdom. What does James 1:5 say we should do if we lack wisdom?

We have seen in the "Going Deeper" section of Day 5 of "Taste" that if we allow God to have His way, suffering develops passion for Christ within us. We have learned in this chapter that if we allow God to have His way through times of chastisement, discernment develops within us. We need to remember these things when we go through trials. The trials may be a direct answer to our prayers to develop passion for Christ and Godly wisdom!

What does Revelation 3:19 say we should do when we are chastised by the Lord?

The King James Version uses the word "zealous." The Greek word for "zealous" is *"zeloo."* According to the Strong's Concordance, this word means "to *have warmth* of feeling for or against: affect, covet (earnestly), (have) desire, (move with) envy, be jealous over, (be) zealous (-ly affect)."[1] Do we actually desire the Lord's chastisement? We will if we remember that it brings peaceful fruits of righteousness in our lives and develops discernment within us if we yield to it. This verse not only tells us to be zealous, but it also tells us to repent. Is there anything currently in your life that the Lord has been chastising you about that you need to repent of? If so, write out a prayer of repentance now. Remember to start it with thankfulness for the chastisement!

Prayer

Oh, most gracious Father, Son and Holy Spirit—the triune God—I love You and desire an intimate relationship with You! I pray that I will have Your perspective on whatever comes my way to develop that intimacy. I know that when intimacy with You begins in my life, I will begin to grow in You. I desire spiritual maturity. I want to be willing to develop that maturity and discernment even though it means that I have to go through times of chastisement. Thank You that Your Word tells me that it is because You love me that You punish me. Thank You also that when You chastise me, it is in a loving, gentle way and not in a condemning way. I pray that You would remind me to guard every gate into my soul and spirit by way of each of my five senses. I will forever be grateful to You for how You have created me with my five senses. I am also thankful for the spiritual aspects each one of them represents and ask You to continue to develop them in my life so that others may see You in me and be drawn to You! In Jesus' precious Name! Amen!

Endnotes

First Things First – Day 1:
[1] "Fetal Development." <u>National Right to Life.</u> 11 April 2006.
< http://www.nrlc.org/abortion/facts/fetaldevelopment.html>

[2] Vine, W.E., et. al. <u>Vine's Complete Expository Dictionary of Old and New Testament Words</u>. Atlanta, GA: Thomas Nelson Publishers. 1984.

First Things First – Day 2:
[1] In the Old Testament, God's people, the Israelites, were slaves in Egypt for a time. God asked Moses to approach Pharoah and ask him to let God's people go. After Pharoah refused to free the Israelites, God sent plagues to Egypt. The last plague was that all the first born would be killed. The Children of Israel were instructed to sacrifice a lamb and place the blood on the door posts. God told them that when He saw the blood on their door posts, He would pass over them and the first born in their homes would not die. Jesus is known for being the perfect "sacrificial lamb" in that He died for our sins on Passover Day, and because of His blood, we have life instead of death!

First Things First – Day 3:
[1] Easton, Burton Scott. "Gate." CD-ROM. ISBE: International Standard Bible Encyclopedia, Database. NavPress, 1998. WORDSearch Bible Study Software. Austin, TX: WORDSearch Corp., 1987-2000.

[2] From Life Application Notes: "The ark (also called the ark of the Testimony or ark of the covenant) was built to hold the Ten Commandments. It symbolized God's covenant with his people. Two gold angels called cherubim were placed on its top. The ark was Israel's most sacred object and was kept in the Most Holy Place in the tabernacle. Only once each year, the high priest entered the Most Holy Place to sprinkle blood on the top of the ark (called the atonement cover) to atone for the sins of the entire nation." Commentary notes on Exodus 37:1. Life Application Bible. Wheaton, IL: Tyndale House Publishers, Inc., 1988, 1989, 1990, 1991.

Taste – Day 2:
[1] "Health, United States, 2004." 2004. Centers for Disease Control and Prevention. 3 June 2007. <www.cdc.gov/nchs/hus.htm>

[2] Bright, Bill. "Your Personal Guide to Fasting and Prayer." 1997. Campus Crusade for Christ. 1997. 11 April 2006. <http://www.bill-bright.com/howtofast/>

Taste – Day 3:
[1] Strong's Greek #3306, Strong's Greek and Hebrew Dictionary, Database. 1990-93 NavPress Software. WORDSearch Bible Study Software. Austin, TX: WORDSearch Corp., 1987-2000.

[2] Strong's Hebrew #3427, Strong's Greek and Hebrew Dictionary, Database. 1990-93 NavPress Software. WORDSearch Bible Study Software. Austin, TX: WORDSearch Corp., 1987-2000.

Taste – Day 5:
[1] Vine, M.E., et. al. An Expository Dictionary of New Testament Words. Old Tappan, NJ: Revell Company, 1966, p. 298

Touch – Day 1:

[1] Smalley, Gary and Trent, John, PhD. The Gift of the Blessing. New York: Inspirational Press, copyright 1991, p. 45

[2] Strong's Greek #5442, <u>Strong's Greek and Hebrew Dictionary</u>, Database. 1990-93 NavPress Software. WORDSearch Bible Study Software. Austin, TX: WORDSearch Corp., 1987-2000.

Touch – Day 2:
[1] Dillow, Linda and Pintus, Lorraine. <u>Intimate Issues</u>. Colorado Springs, CO: Waterbrook Press, copyright 1999, p. 86

Touch – Day 3:
[1] Swindoll, Luci. <u>God Always Has a Plan B</u>. Grand Rapids, MI: Zondervan Corporation, copyright 1999, p. 93

Touch – Day 4:
Touch – Day 4:
[1] "The apple of my eye." <u>The Phrase Finder</u>. Gary Martin. 4 June 2007. <www.phrases.org.uk/meanings/34850.htm>
Touch – Day 5:
[1] Murray, Andrew. <u>With Christ in the School of Prayer</u>. North Brunswick, NJ: Bridge-Logos publishers, revised by Harold J. Chadwick, 1999, p. 2

Sight – Day 1:
[1] Ankerberg, Dr. John and Weldon, Dr. John. "The Evolution of Life, Probability Considerations and Common Sense – Part 3." <u>Ankerberg Theological Research Institute</u>. 11 April 2006 <www.johnankerberg. org>

Sight – Day 2:
[1] Weiss, Daniel. "Pornography: Harmless Fun or Public Health Hazard? Testimony at the May 19, 2005 summit on pornography and violence against women and children" <u>Focus on the Family</u>. 11 April 2006 <www.family.org>

[2] "Help for Struggling Christian Leaders," copyright 1999 by Focus on the Family, Colorado Springs, CO., <www.pureintimacy.org>

[3] Arterburn, Steve and Stoeker, Fred. <u>Every Man's Battle</u>. Colorado Springs, CO: WaterBrook Press, 2000.

Sight – Day 3:
[1] Banks, Robert and Stevens, R. Paul Stevens. <u>Complete Book of Everyday Christianity</u>. Downers Grove, IL: InterVarsity Press, 1997

Sight – Day 5:
[1] Chapman, Steven Curtis and Naish, Phil. "More to This Life." 1989. Sparrow Song (a div. of EMI Christian Music Publishing) / Careers - BMG Music Publishing, Inc. (BMI) / BMG Songs, Inc / Beckengus Music (Admin. by BMG Music Publishing) / Greg Nelson Music / Pamela Kay Music

[2] Thomas, Daman, et. al. "More to Life." 2003. E Two Music, Demis Hot Songs, First Ave. Music, The Lady Roars, Slow Guy Songs, Diesel Liesel.

[3] From Operation Mobilization's website, www.om.org on April 10, 2004. [OM's source - World Christian Trends, David Barrett & Todd Johnson www.gem-werc,org/gd/gd.htm]

Hearing – Day 5:
[1] Strong's Greek #5287, <u>Strong's Greek and Hebrew Dictionary</u>, Database. 1990-93 NavPress Software. WORDSearch Bible Study Software. Austin, TX: WORDSearch Corp., 1987-2000.

[2] Strong's Greek #5259, <u>Strong's Greek and Hebrew Dictionary</u>, Database. 1990-93 NavPress Software. WORDSearch Bible Study Software. Austin, TX: WORDSearch Corp., 1987-2000.

[3] Strong's Greek #2476, <u>Strong's Greek and Hebrew Dictionary</u>, Database. 1990-93 NavPress Software. WORDSearch Bible Study Software. Austin, TX: WORDSearch Corp., 1987-2000.

Smell – Day 1:
[1] Alvin, Virginia and Silverstein, Robert. <u>Smell, the Subtle Sense</u>. New York: Morrow Junior Books, 1992

Smell – Day 2:
[1] Cymbala, Jim. <u>Fresh Wind, Fresh Fire</u>. Grand Rapids, MI: Zondervan Publishing House. 1997, p. 142-143.

[2] "Fact Sheet: Respiratory Health Effects of Passive Smoking." <u>United States Environmental Protection Agency</u>. January, 1993, updated 20 March 2007 <http://www.epa.gov/smokefree/pubs/etsfs.html>

[3] Staten, Clark. "Youths Die By Inhaling Household Substances." 1996. <u>Emergency Response and Research Institute</u>. 21 October 2004. <www.emergency.com/inhalnt.htm>

Smell – Day 4:
[1] McVey, Steve. <u>Grace Walk</u>. Eugene, OR: Harvest House Publishers. 1995, p.70

Smell – Day 5:
[1] Strong's Greek #2206, <u>Strong's Greek and Hebrew Dictionary</u>, Database. 1990-93 NavPress Software. WORDSearch Bible Study Software. Austin, TX: WORDSearch Corp., 1987-2000.

Bibliography

Alvin, Virginia and Silverstein, Robert. <u>Smell, the Subtle Sense</u>.
New York: Morrow Junior Books, 1992.

Ankerberg, Dr. John and Weldon, Dr. John. "The Evolution of Life,
Probability Considerations and Common Sense – Part 3."
<u>Ankerberg Theological Research Institute</u>. 11 April 2006
<u><www.johnankerberg.org></u>

Arterburn, Steve and Stoeker, Fred. <u>Every Man's Battle</u>. Colorado
Springs, CO; WaterBrook Press, 2000.

Banks, Robert and Stevens, R. Paul Stevens. <u>Complete Book of
Everyday Christianity</u>. Downers Grove, IL: InterVarsity
Press, 1997.

Bright, Bill. "Your Personal Guide to Fasting and Prayer."
<u>Campus Crusade for Christ</u>. 1997. <http://www.billbright.
com/howtofast/>

<u>Come to Your Senses – Think Quest</u>. 7 June 2007. "Your Sense of
Touch." 23 March 2004. <<u>http://library.thinkquest.org/3750/
touch/touch.html</u>>

Cymbala, Jim. <u>Fresh Wind, Fresh Fire</u>. Grand Rapids, MI: Zondervan
Publishing House. 1997.

Dillow, Linda and Pintus, Lorraine. <u>Intimate Issues</u>. Colorado Springs, CO: Waterbrook Press, 1999.

"Fact Sheet: Respiratory Health Effects of Passive Smoking." <u>United States Environmental Protection Agency</u>. January, 1993, updated 20 March 2007 <http://www.epa.gov/smoke-free/pubs/etsfs.html>

"Health, United States, 2004." 2004. <u>Centers for Disease Control and Prevention</u>. 3 June 2007. <www.cdc.gov/nchs/hus.htm>

"Help for Struggling Christian Leaders," copyright 1999 by Focus on the Family, Colorado Springs, CO. <u><www.pureintimacy.org></u>

<u>How Stuff Works</u>. 1998-2007. Brain, Marshal. 24 April 2004. Atlanta, GA. <http://www.howstuffworks.com/>

International Standard Bible Encyclopedia, Database. CD-ROM. NavPress, 1998. WORDSearch Bible Study Software. Austin, TX: WORDSearch Corp., 1987-2000.

<u>Kimball's Biology Pages</u>. 25 February 2007. Kimball, John W. PhD. 19 March 2004. <http://users.rcn.com/jkimball.ma.ultranet/BiologyPages/W/Welcome.html>

<u>Life Application Bible</u>. Wheaton, IL: Tyndale House Publishers, Inc., 1988, 1989, 1990, 1991.

Martin, Gary. "The apple of my eye." <u>The Phrase Finder</u>. 4 June 2007. <www.phrases.org.uk/meanings/34850.htm>

McVey, Steve. <u>Grace Walk</u>. Eugene, OR: Harvest House Publishers. 1995.

Murray, Andrew. With Christ in the School of Prayer. North Brunswick, NJ: Bridge-Logos publishers, revised by Harold J. Chadwick, 1999.

National Right to Life. 11 April 2006. <http://www.nrlc.org>

Nueroscience for Kids. 6 June 2007. Chudler, Eric H. PhD. 19 March 2004. <http://faculty.washington.edu/chudler/neurok.html >

Operation Mobilization. Article on Evangelism Statistics. 10 April 2004. <www.om.org> [OM's source - World Christian Trends, David Barrett & Todd Johnson www. gem-werc,org/gd/gd.htm]

Probert Encyclopaedia. 1993-2007. Probert, Matt and Leela. 19 March 2004. <http://www.probert-encyclopaedia.co.uk/>

Smalley, Gary and Trent, John, PhD. The Gift of the Blessing. New York: Inspirational Press, 1991.

Staten, Clark. "Youths Die By Inhaling Household Substances." 1996. Emergency Response and Research Institute. 21 October 2004. <www.emergency.com/inhalnt.htm>

Strong's Greek and Hebrew Dictionary, Database © 1990-93 NavPress Software. WORDSearch Bible Study Software. Austin, TX: WORDSearch Corp., 1987-2000.

Swindoll, Luci. God Always Has a Plan B. Grand Rapids, MI: Zondervan Corporation, copyright 1999.

Tim Jacob Smell Research Laboratory. 26 March 2007. Jacob, Tim. 19 March 2004. <http://www.cf.ac.uk/biosi/staff/jacob/index. html >

Vine, W.E., et. al. <u>Vine's Complete Expository Dictionary of Old and New Testament Words</u>. Atlanta, GA: Thomas Nelson Publishers. 1984.

Weiss, Daniel. "Pornography: Harmless Fun or Public Health Hazard? Testimony at the May 19, 2005 summit on pornography and violence against women and children" <u>Focus on the Family</u>. 11 April 2006 <www.family.org>

We would love to hear how God has used *Loving God With All Five Senses* in your life! Let us know by contacting us via our website, www.legacyministries.info.

You may also contact us through our website to:

- Find out more information about how Legacy Ministries can help you or your church.

- Order DVD's or CD's of Tammy speaking about *Loving God With All Five Senses* or other topics.

- Find out about booking Tammy to speak for your event.

Tammy Melton is the founder of Legacy Ministries for Christ, Incorporated in Fayetteville, GA. Legacy Ministries offers resources to individuals in the body of Christ, local church bodies, and the interdenominational church as a whole to be trained and equipped for ministry.

Printed in the United States
215691BV00001B/3/A